Instant Manipulatives for Math

Alison Abrohms

SCHOLASTIC
PROFESSIONAL BOOKS

New York • Toronto • London • Auckland • Sydney

To Alyssa Lauren and Megan Faith,
for all your love.

Cover design by Vincent Ceci
Book design by Nancy Metcalf
Illustration by Lynn Vineyard

ISBN 0-590-49238-1

ontents

continued

Put animals, insects, and outer space at your students' fingertips—with activities that enhance your math program. *1001 Instant Manipulatives for Math*, a book bursting with multipurpose reproducible manipulatives and activities, lets you do just that.

Explore sorting, classifying, patterning, adding and subtracting, graphing, measurement, time, fractions, and more with six special units in **Section 1**. In addition to a range of manipulatives and suggested activities, you'll find 10 reproducible story mats—from a farm setting to an outer space environment. As children combine manipulatives and story mats in creative displays, they'll also be hard at work using mathematical concepts and understanding to solve problems.

Section 2 introduces math materials such as attribute pieces, pattern shapes, pentominoes, place value models, number cards, spinners, number cubes, and coins. Many of the suggested activities reflect the Curriculum and Evaluation Standards for School Mathematics (NCTM, 1989) and can be adapted to meet your classroom needs.

Activities in both sections often suggest that children paste manipulatives in place to create records of their solutions. When collected over time in student portfolios, this work can give you, your students, and their families a clear picture of growth and achievement.

Preparing to Use the Manipulatives

Prepare sets of manipulatives as you need them for individual activities or for long-term units. Let students cut apart and color their own manipulatives and store them in labeled envelopes or resealable plastic bags for ongoing use in the classroom. (This storage system makes it easier for children to share their manipulatives at home, too.)

Prepare a set of manipulatives for your use, as well as a set that students can use at a math center. Laminate these manipulatives for durability. Apply felt backing to any manipulatives for use on flannel boards. For demonstration purposes or large group work, copy manipulatives onto transparencies and use with an overhead projector.

Suggested activities allow for flexible grouping, including whole class instruction, individual work, and cooperative learning with two or more students. For activities that require more of any one manipulative than is included on a page, small groups of students might work together, pooling their cutouts.

Finally, before the guided activities get under way, give children time to explore the manipulatives on their own. Because the cutouts are child-size, personal, interesting, and diverse, children will naturally be drawn to observe, touch, position, and reposition their new math tools. After all, that's what math manipulatives are all about!

section **1**

Animals, insects, natural objects, people, vehicles, buildings, houses, food, toys, and seasonal objects are just some of the manipulatives you'll find in this section—and all are perfect for practicing a wide variety of math concepts. Below, you'll find strategies for using any of the manipulatives in Section 1 to teach common mathematical concepts and skills. More specific activities introduce each unit. All can be adapted to meet your students' needs, and as you use them over and over, you're sure to discover your own ideas, too. Finally, the story mats in this section (see pages 61-72) make math discovery even more fun. You can use the suggested activities for each story mat to encourage children's communication and problem-solving skills.

Sorting and Classifying

As children observe their surroundings, they learn to identify attributes of the objects in their world, such as short, tall, red, blue, yellow, round, square, toy, and clothes. Sorting by attribute or property is a basic thinking skill that underlies such concepts as patterning, geometry, graphing, and measurement.

Children can use the manipulatives in this section to sort and classify. For example, ask students to show:

○ animals that fly and animals that don't fly

○ animals that swim and animals that don't swim

○ animals that live on a farm and those animals that do not

○ vehicles with wheels and vehicles without wheels

○ foods children like and foods they do not like

○ foods that are fruits and vegetables and other foods

○ objects that are longer than a pencil and objects that are shorter than a pencil

After children sort objects into sets, ask key questions such as: "What rules did you use to sort the objects?" "How are the objects in this group alike?" "How are the groups different?" "Does this object belong in your groups?" "Can you show another way to sort these objects?" "What name can you give this group of objects?"

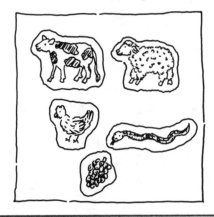

As children become proficient in identifying attributes, encourage them to use logical thought processes to identify a picture. For example, display these manipulatives:

Give children clues to help them eliminate pictures until only one remains. For example:

○ I am thinking of an animal. (eliminates pine cone)

○ This is a farm animal. (eliminates snake)

○ The animal does not lay eggs. (eliminates chicken)

○ The animal gives wool. (eliminates cow)

○ What is the animal? (sheep)

Patterning

As children gain skill in identifying attributes such as shape, size, color, and position, they will begin to recognize patterns based on those attributes. Children may also discover more inherent patterns, such as those that relate to objects' uses. The manipulatives in this section provide an unending array of patterning possibilities. As children use the manipulatives, they may spontaneously form some of their own patterns. You may also want to create pattern cards for children to copy and extend, for example:

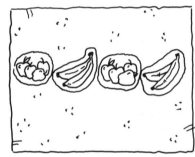  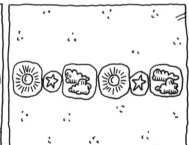

As children form patterns, ask key questions such as: "How would you read this pattern?" "What would you put next in this pattern?" "And after that?" "Can you make another pattern that is like this one?" "How are the patterns alike?"

Graphing

Graphing is a useful recording device for organizing and presenting information. Graphing opportunities may spring from many of the sorting activities. Children can make picture graphs by pasting their groupings on paper, or color to record observations on a bar graph.

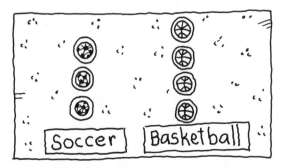 

Ask children questions about their graphs, such as: "Which column has more (less, most, least)?" "Are there any columns that have the same?" "What does the graph tell you?"

Number Concepts

From early readiness skills to more sophisticated concepts, you can use Section 1 manipulatives in many number-related activities. Suggestions include:

○ Ask children to make a set of chicks and a set of eggs that have the same number (more, fewer), then compare sets by matching elements one to one.

○ Display a number card. Ask children to show a set that matches the number.

○ Let children form their own sets and use dot cards, picture cards, or number cards to label the sets.

○ Ask children to display a set of 5, then show a set with one more (two more), one less (two less), and so on.

○ Ask children to make a line of 10 animals (people, objects, and so on) and identify the ordinal positions.

○ Have children arrange manipulatives in sets of 2 (3, 4, 5), then skip count.

○ Invite children to create stories and use the manipulatives to model or act out the situations.

Computation

As children begin early computation work, modeling helps them understand the processes. They can use manipulatives in this section to model addition, subtraction, multiplication, and division situations. Some computation problems to get you started include:

○ Two birds are in a tree. One more bird takes a break on a branch. How many birds are there now?

○ Eight pine cones fell to the ground. James and Phoebe picked up one in each of their hands. How many are left on the ground?

○ Mrs. Castle has 6 windows on each floor of her house. She has 3 floors. How many windows are in Mrs. Castle's house?

○ A pizza has 12 slices. Four friends want to share the pizza equally. How many slices will each friend get?

Animals

Here are some suggestions for using the manipulatives in this unit:

○ Give pairs of children some or all of the animals in this unit. Encourage children to talk about the animals and describe any characteristics they notice. Then have children classify the animals in sets and explain how they created their groups.

○ As you name some animals, ask children to display them on a sheet of construction paper. Say, for example, "Show a sheep, a goat, a goose, a pony, and a cow on the grass. Count to find how many animals are in the field." "Count to find how many animals have four legs."

○ For work with ordinal numbers, give children a sheet of paper and ask them to draw a tree on the left side. Have them position the animals by following these directions: The meadow animals are in line behind the tree. The squirrel is first in line. The owl is behind the squirrel. The beaver is next in line. The duck is last. Ask: "Which animal is second in line?" "Which animal is fourth in line?" Invite children to continue by describing other arrangements for their classmates to try.

○ Paste 10 pairs of animals on index cards. Small groups of children can mix the cards, arrange them face down in two rows, then take turns choosing two cards, looking for a match. If no match is found, the cards are returned face down in the same location. Play continues until all matches are found.

○ Give pairs of children number cards (see pages 89-90). One child can display a number card while the other child shows that many animals on the sorting mat (see page 63).

○ Ask small groups of children to sort animals into categories and then make graphs to show the animal sets they form.

○ Attach felt strips to the backs of some animal cutouts. Display animals on the flannel board and tell number stories for children to solve. For example: A cow, a calf, and a collie live on a farm. They find a calico cat with four kittens. How many animals live on the farm?

○ Ask children to write their own number stories for classmates to solve. The children can read their stories aloud as they model them at the flannel board.

○ Ask children to compare a group of animals, then paste them on paper in order from largest to smallest. Display papers on a Big to Little bulletin board.

Ideas for using these manipulatives with story mats are provided in the Story Mats unit (see pages 61-72).

Farm Animals

turkey

rooster

goat

lamb

sheep

chicken

chick

goose

gosling

pig

piglet

cow

calf

egg

egg

egg

Pets

collie puppy

calico

calico kitten

collie

tabby

tabby kitten

hound

hound puppy

mouse

horse

pony

mouse

Meadow Animals

squirrel

owl

bat

robin

blue jay

eagle

duck

duckling

beaver

snake

Woodland Animals

frog

toad

fox

fox

porcupine

rabbit

rabbit

skunk

rabbit

rabbit

raccoon

Jungle and Forest Animals

tiger

deer

peacock

lion

zebra

kangaroo

Jungle Animals

gorilla

rhinoceros

ostrich

monkey

giraffe

elephant

Water Creatures

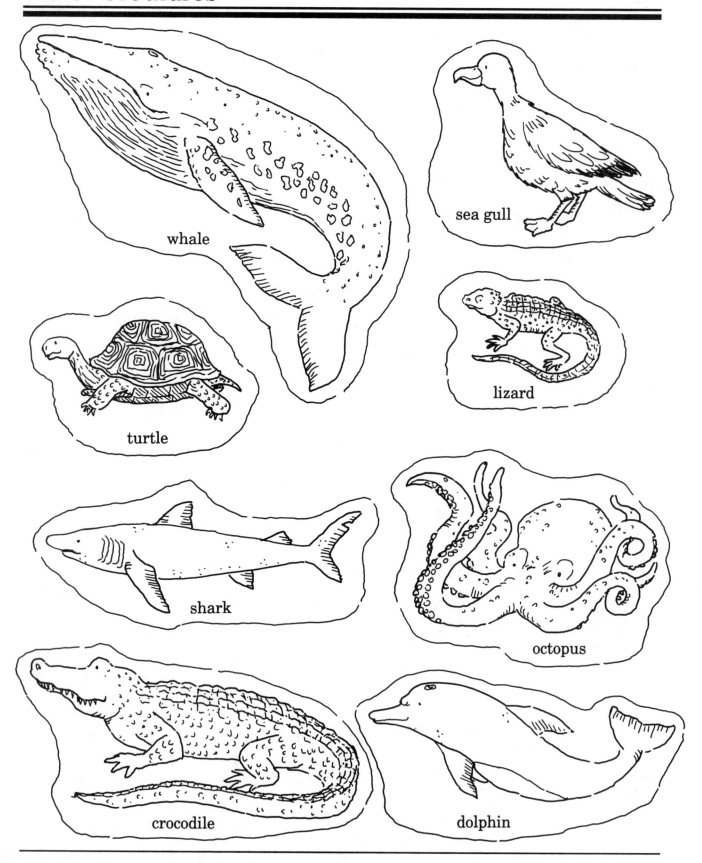

whale

sea gull

turtle

lizard

shark

octopus

crocodile

dolphin

Water Creatures

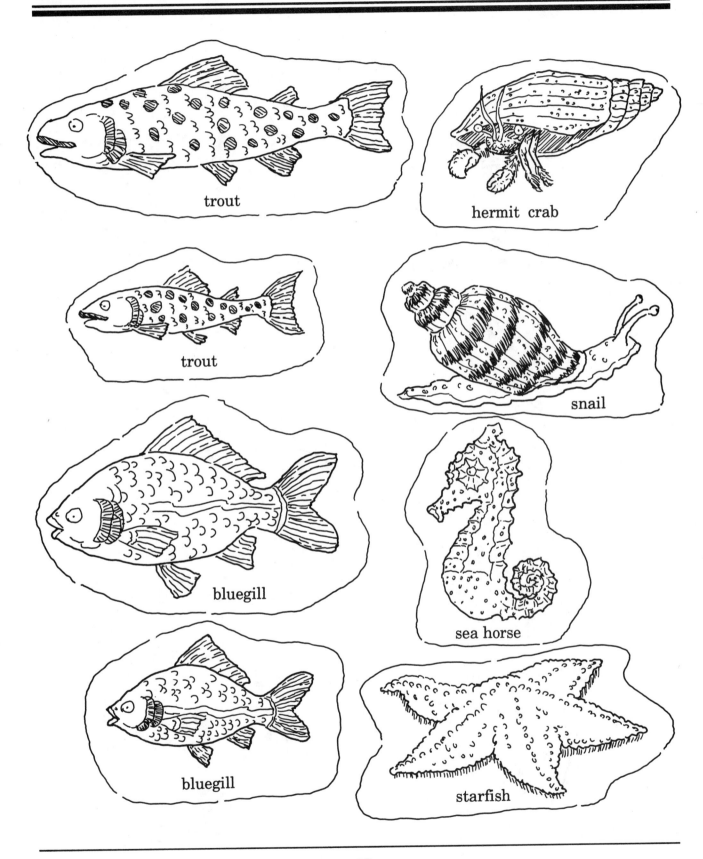

trout

hermit crab

trout

snail

bluegill

sea horse

bluegill

starfish

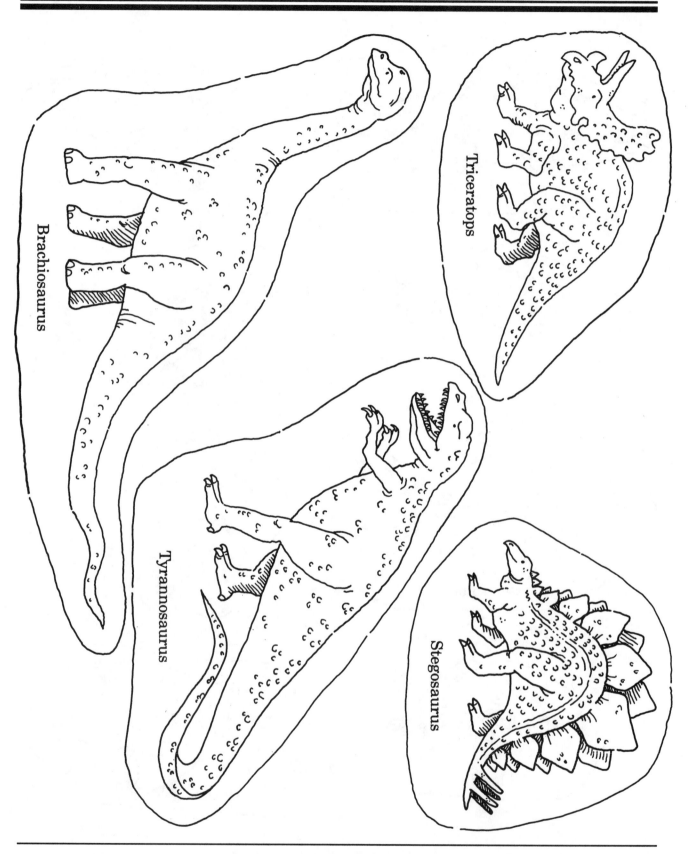

Insects and Nature

Here are some suggestions for using the manipulatives in this unit:

❍ Provide small groups of children with the insect cutouts (see pages 22-24). Encourage children to examine the insects and identify any that they recognize. Children can experiment with sorting the insects into sets and explain their groupings for the class.

❍ Provide paper, paste, and multiple copies of a few insect pages for each child. Children can paste the insects on paper to form patterns.

Working in pairs, children can extend their partners' patterns.

❍ Children can combine flowers and other objects to create gardens, then tell story problems about their pictures. For example, "There are 6 roses and 6 tulips in my garden. How many flowers are there?"

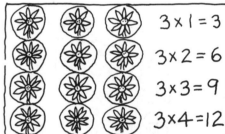

❍ Children can paste flowers (see page 25) in arrays to form multiplication tables, then write multiplication sentences next to each row in the array.

❍ Paste felt strips on insects (see pages 22-24) and display a set on the flannel board (for example, 4 butterflies and 2 grasshoppers). Ask questions that require children to find fractional parts of the sets: "What part of the set is butterflies?" (4/6 or 2/3) "What part of the set is grasshoppers?" (2/6 or 1/3)

❍ Give each child an inch ruler (see page 103). Challenge children to find objects in the room that measure 12 inches. Once children are familiar with this measure, ask them to paste butterflies in rows, end to end, until they have made rows that they think measure about 12 inches. Children can use the rulers to check their estimates.

❍ Give each child a copy of the cube cutout (see page 94) and three copies of two kinds of flowers (see page 25), such as 3 roses and 3 tulips. Have children paste one flower on each side of their cubes, then assemble. Children can toss the cubes, tallying how many times each kind of flower lands on top. Before they begin the toss, encourage children to predict how many times each flower will land on top in 10 or 20 tries.

Ideas on using these manipulatives with the story mats are provided in the Story Mats unit (see pages 61-72).

Butterflies

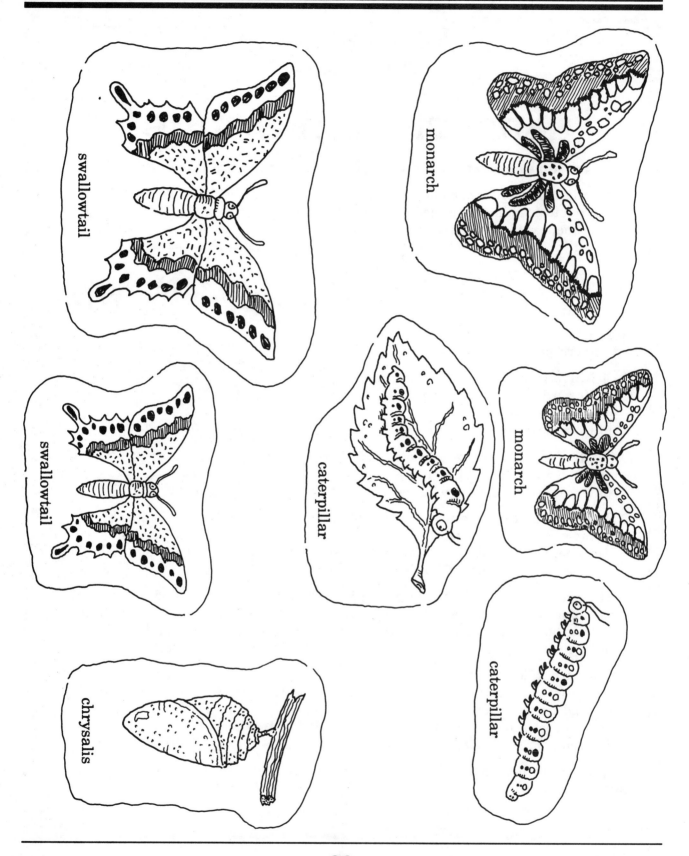

swallowtail

monarch

swallowtail

caterpillar

monarch

chrysalis

caterpillar

Insects

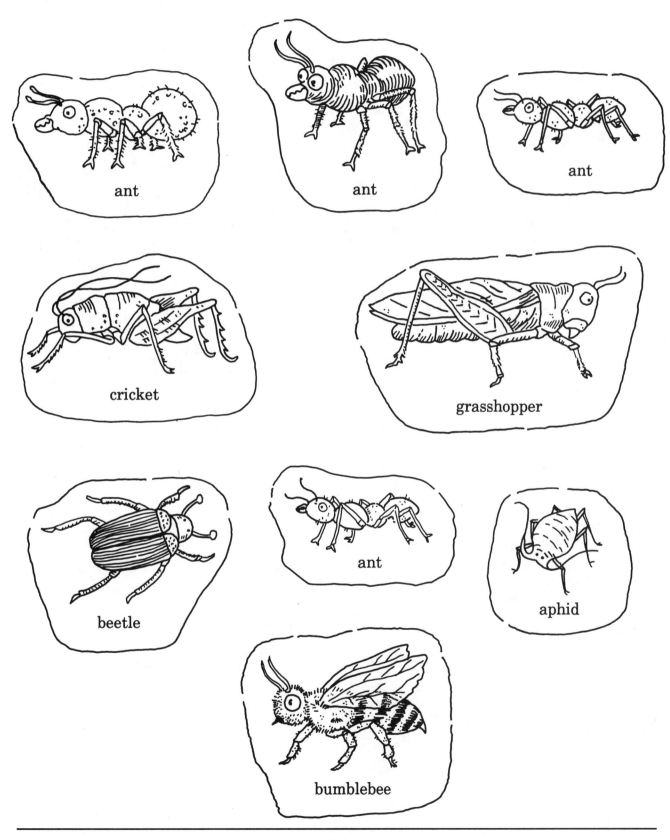

ant

ant

ant

cricket

grasshopper

beetle

ant

aphid

bumblebee

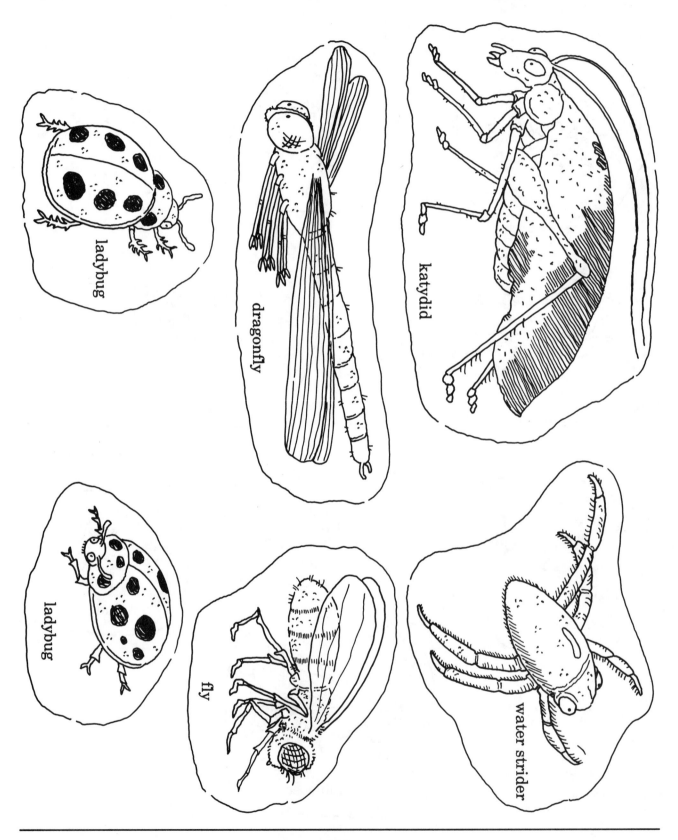

ladybug

dragonfly

katydid

ladybug

fly

water strider

Flowers

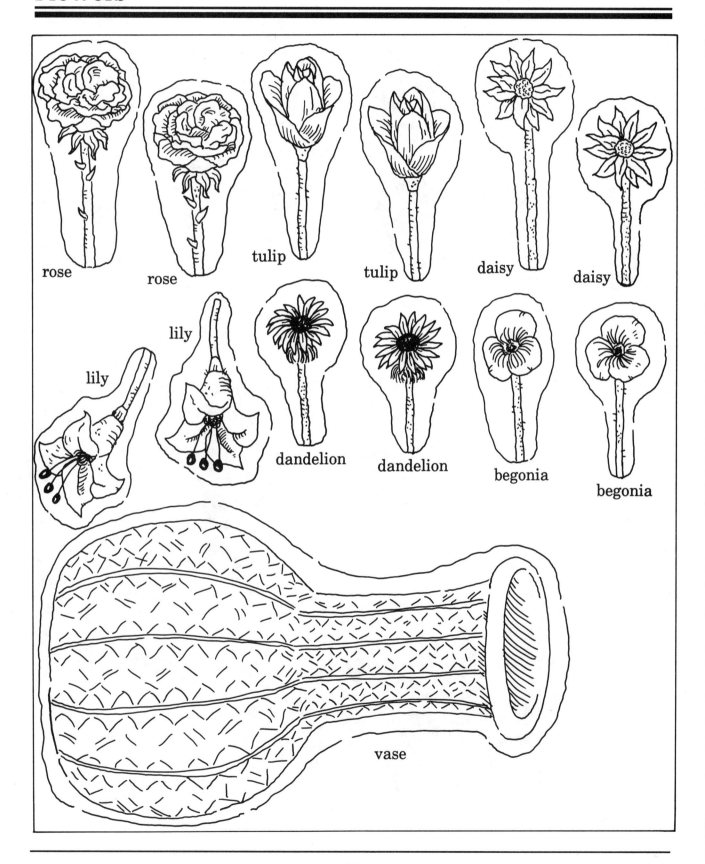

rose

rose

tulip

tulip

daisy

daisy

lily

lily

dandelion

dandelion

begonia

begonia

vase

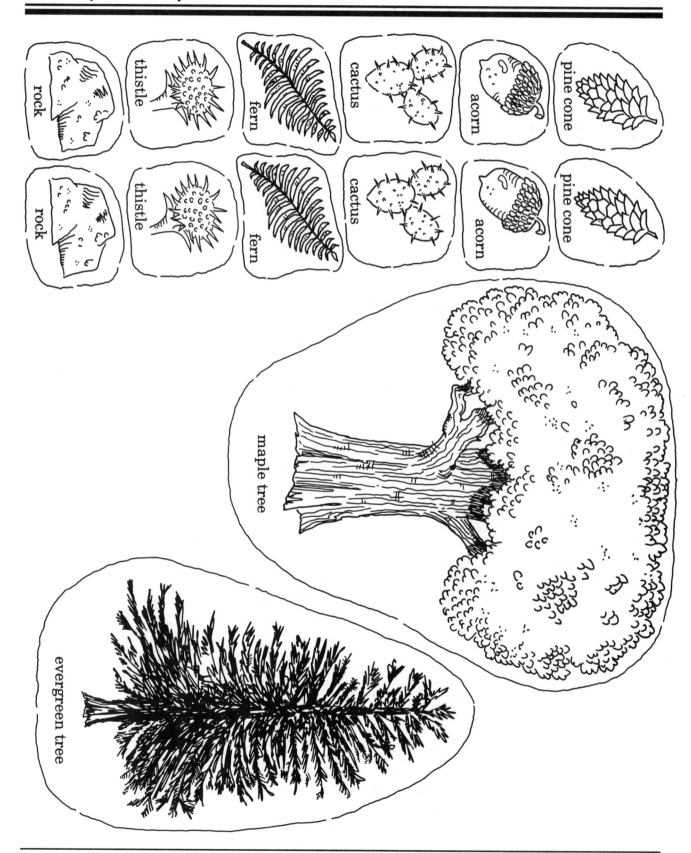

rock

thistle

fern

cactus

acorn

pine cone

rock

thistle

fern

cactus

acorn

pine cone

maple tree

evergreen tree

Leaves

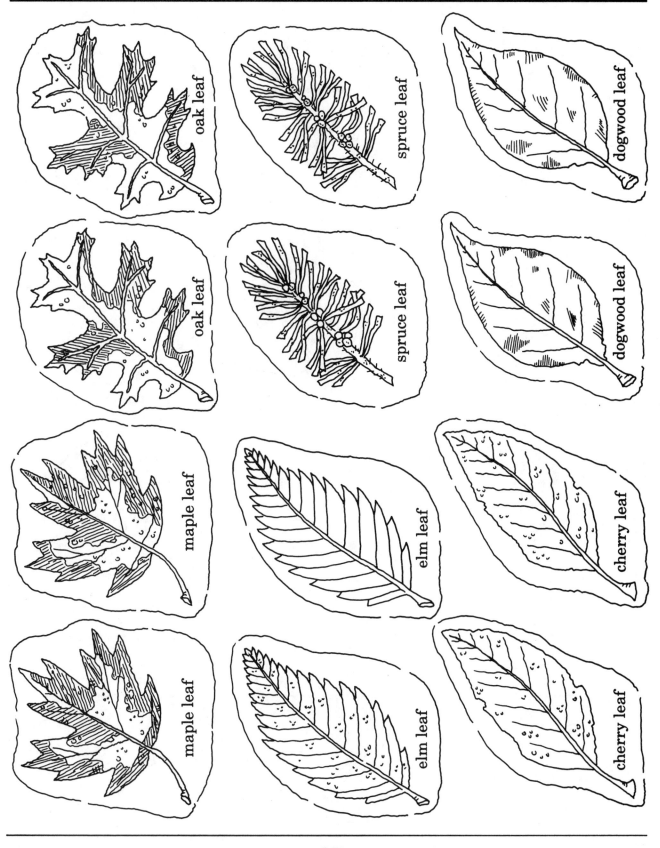

oak leaf

spruce leaf

dogwood leaf

oak leaf

spruce leaf

dogwood leaf

maple leaf

elm leaf

cherry leaf

maple leaf

elm leaf

cherry leaf

Shells

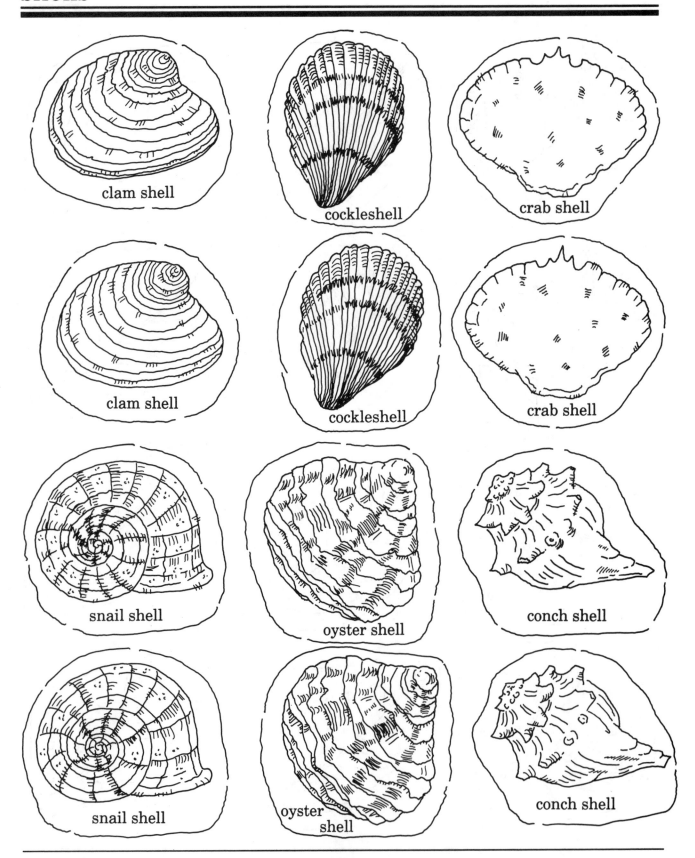

clam shell

cockleshell

crab shell

clam shell

cockleshell

crab shell

snail shell

oyster shell

conch shell

snail shell

oyster
shell

conch shell

People, Transportation, and Neighborhoods

Here are some suggestions for using the manipulatives in this unit:

○ Give children strips of paper and ask them to paste houses and buildings (see pages 37-38) in a row. Practice ordinal positions by giving children directions such as: "Draw a flower in front of the second building. Draw a dog in front of the fifth building." Let children add their own directions for classmates to follow.

○ Make transparencies of graph paper (see page 106-107) and buildings (see pages 37-38). Place buildings such as houses, apartment buildings, a school, and a library on graph paper to form a neighborhood map. Using the overhead projector, ask children to find distances between buildings by counting squares on the graph paper. Or, have children practice giving and following directions such as, "Start at the library. Move left 6 spaces and up 9 spaces. Where are you?"

○ Practice positional terms on a flannel board. Attach felt strips to vehicles (see pages 35-36). Place several vehicles in line on the flannel board.

Give children directions such as: "Place a minivan in front of the bus." "Place a helicopter in front of the minivan."

○ Let small groups of children attach sticks to some figures to make puppets. Children can use number cards to show addition and subtraction sentences, then model the actions with the puppets.

Ideas for using these manipulatives with story mats are provided in the Story Mats unit (see pages 61-72).

Occupations

business person

teacher

writer

farmer

Occupations

construction worker

musician

firefighter

police officer

doctor

mail carrier

artist

chef

Children

Vehicles

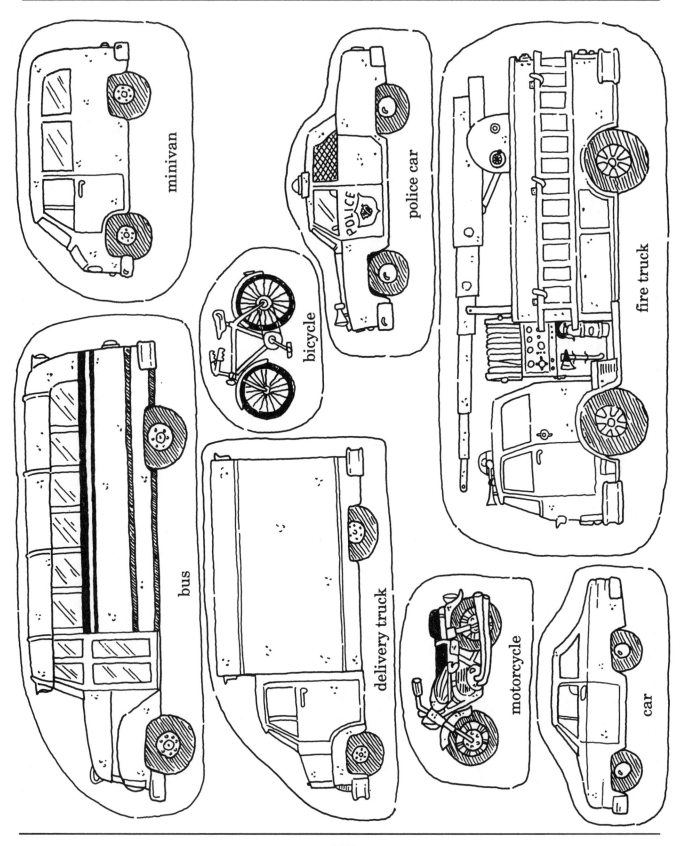

minivan

police car

fire truck

bicycle

bus

delivery truck

motorcycle

car

Vehicles

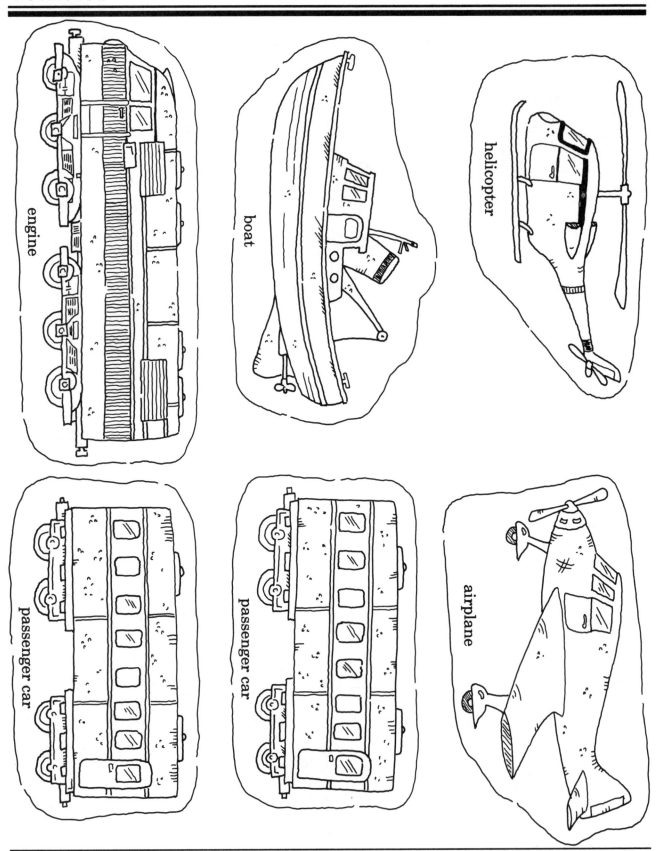

engine

boat

helicopter

passenger car

passenger car

airplane

Homes

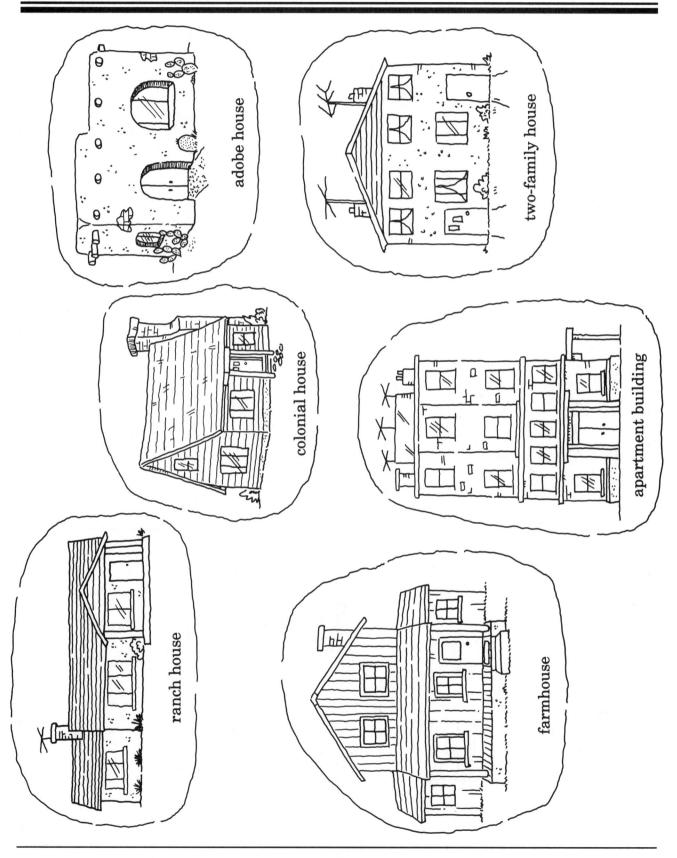

adobe house

two-family house

colonial house

apartment building

ranch house

farmhouse

Buildings

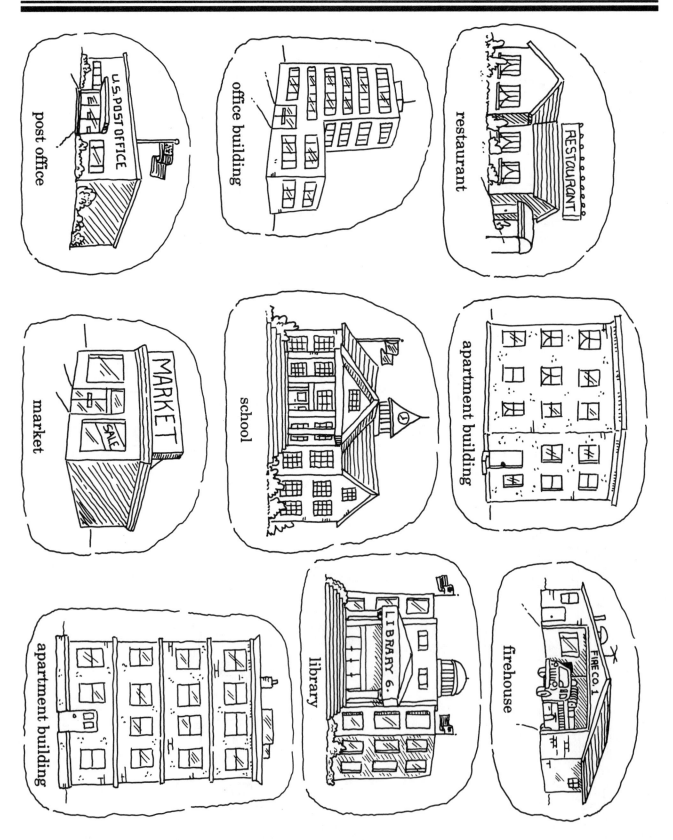

post office

office building

restaurant

market

school

apartment building

apartment building

library

firehouse

Food, Toys, Sports, and Musical Instruments

Here are some suggestions for using the manipulatives in this unit:

○ Attach felt strips to 10 pieces of fruit (see page 40), 10 toys, (see pages 43-44), and 10 musical instruments (see pages 47-48). Place all the objects on a flannel board. Begin to form a set of fruit by slowly moving one piece at a time into the center of the flannel board. Tell children, "I am forming a set. Who can add more objects to my set?" Invite volunteers to add fruit to the set, then ask: "What name can we give this set?" (fruit) Move the fruit back to the side of the flannel board, then form sets with toys and instruments.

○ Place felt strips on 6 foods (see pages 40-42). Place the foods on a flannel board, and ask children to choose their favorite foods. Volunteers can tally children's responses. Together, record the data on a graph (see page 72).

○ Children can arrange 20 (or more) pieces of fruit in sets of two, then skip count by 2. Provide children with hundreds charts (see page 91) and have them color each number they say as they count by 2. At another time, repeat the activity, counting by 3, by 4, and by 5.

○ Using any of the manipulatives in this unit, children can work in pairs to practice visual estimation skills. In turn, children display manipulatives as their partners estimate whether the amount is more than 5 (or than 10) or less than 5 (or 10). Partners can count together to check estimates.

○ Give children the people cutouts (see pages 30-34) and some of the sports equipment (see pages 45-46). Give directions such as: "The girl wearing shorts has three baseballs. The fire fighter has seven whistles." Children can place the corresponding number of objects next to each person, paste their responses in place, and write or dictate sentences that describe their pictures.

○ Give small groups of children a spinner labeled 1 to 4 (see page 120) and manipulatives from this unit. In turn, children can spin, then take that many manipulatives from a pile. The first child to get 20 manipulatives can them and challenge classmates to figure out the rule for grouping.

Ideas for using these manipulatives with story mats are provided in the Story Mats unit (see pages 61-72).

Fruits

apples

bananas

pears

grapes

strawberries

lemons

oranges

pineapple

watermelon

peaches

Vegetables

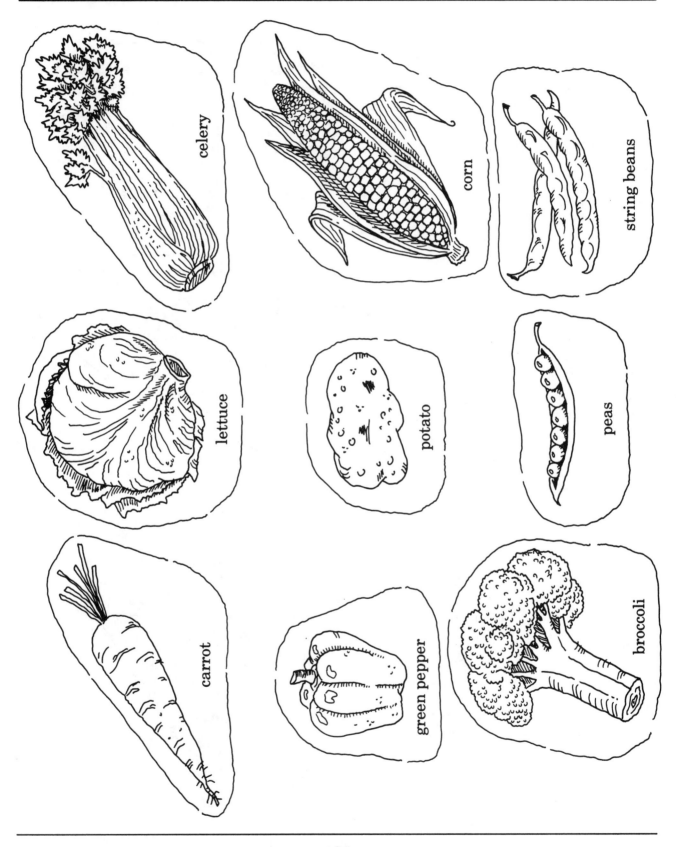

celery

corn

string beans

lettuce

potato

peas

carrot

green pepper

broccoli

Food

juice

hamburger

peanut butter and jelly sandwich

milk

hot dog

raisins

cookie

popcorn

pizza

Toys

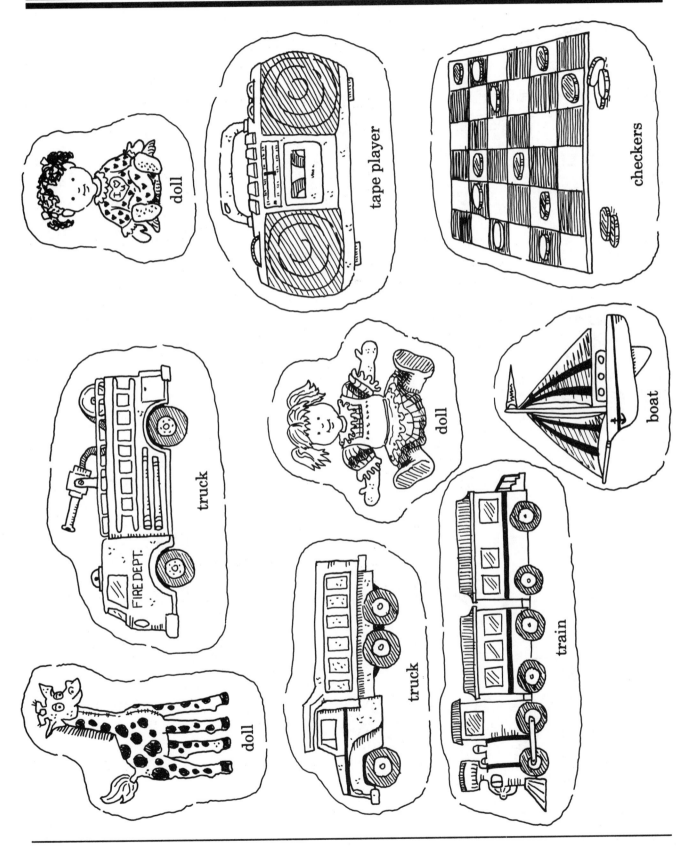

doll

tape player

checkers

truck

doll

boat

truck

doll

train

Toys

radio

teddy bear

Picture Puzzle

puzzle

coloring book

Daisy

Tulip...

game

crayons

CRAYONS

game

blocks

bubbles and wand

Mr. Bubble

Sports

basketball

baseball

soccer

roller skating

swimming

skiing

Sports

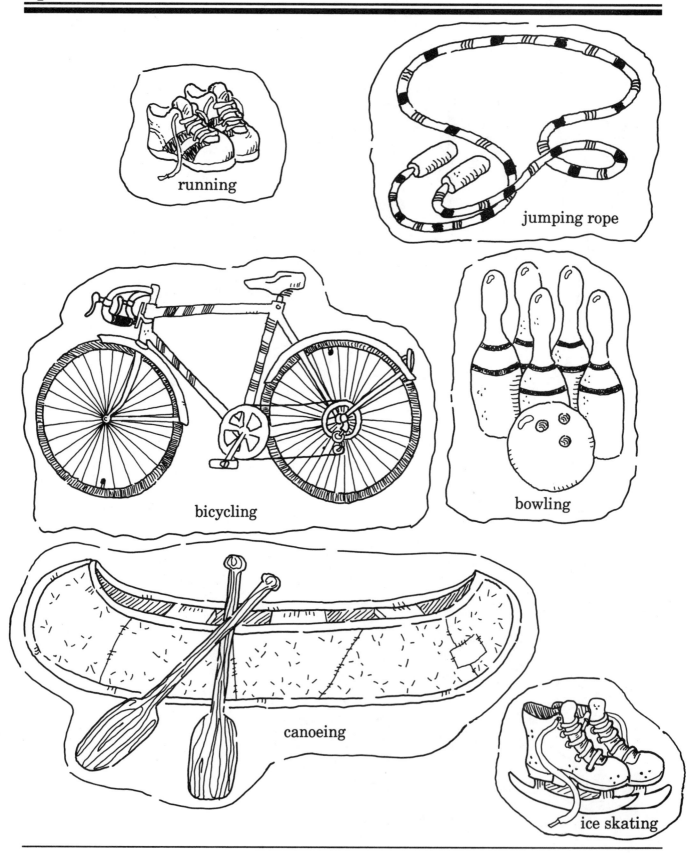

running

jumping rope

bicycling

bowling

canoeing

ice skating

Musical Instruments

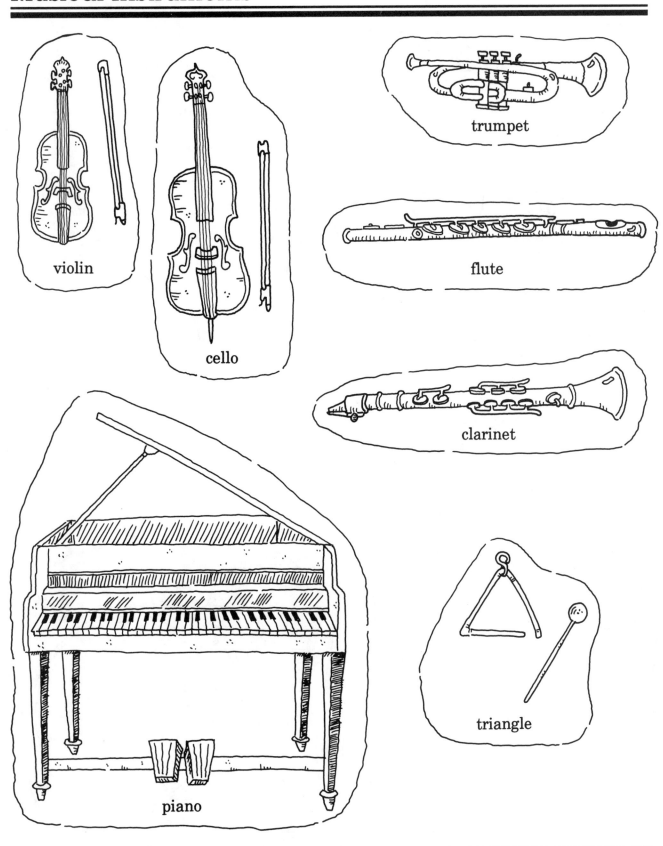

violin

cello

trumpet

flute

clarinet

piano

triangle

Musical Instruments

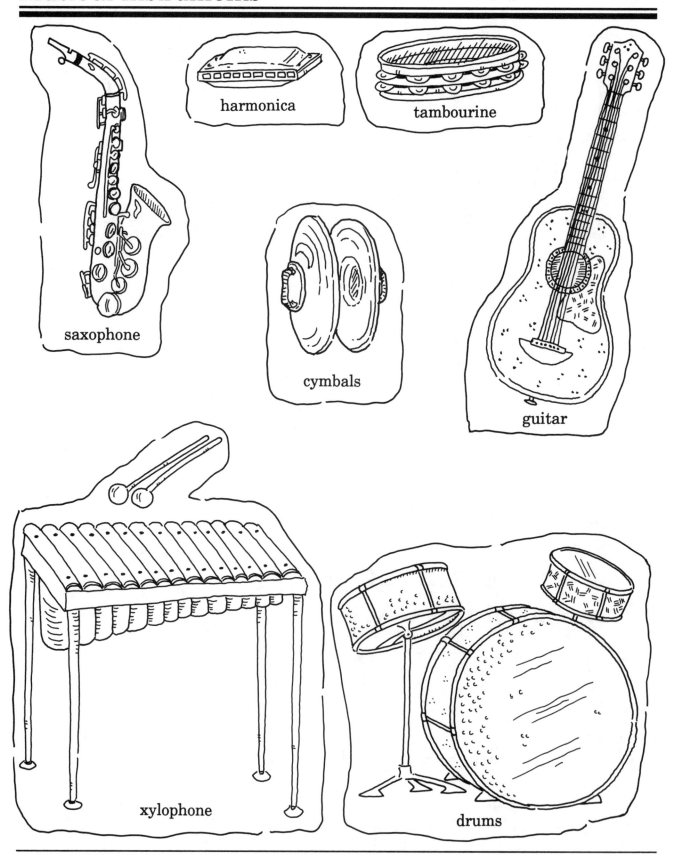

harmonica

tambourine

saxophone

cymbals

guitar

xylophone

drums

Weather and Space

Here are some suggestions for using the manipulatives in this unit:

○ Children can cut out each of the large snowflakes (see page 51), then fold the snowflakes into two equal parts to determine if the snowflakes are symmetrical.

○ Make a class temperature time line with the weather scenes (see page 50) and thermometers (see page 105). At the same time each day, have children use an outdoor thermometer to determine the temperature, then record the information by coloring in the reproducible thermometer. Have children select the appropriate weather scene each day, then paste that picture and the thermometer to a piece of paper. Post the pictures in a row to show temperature and weather changes over time.

○ Use weather scenes (see page 51) to create pictures that are not logical. For example, put a snowman in the scene of a hot day. Show children in shorts in the scene of a cold day. Challenge children to identify what is wrong, then switch manipulatives to make pictures that make sense. (Use a flannel board to allow children to make changes easily.)

○ Make space dominoes by pasting number cards (see pages 89-90) and space objects (see page 52) on rectangular pieces of paper. Children can play dominoes by matching the numbers and objects as they lay the cards end to end.

○ Children can make models of the solar system using the sun, the planets, and stars (see page 52). Ask children to count to tell how many planets and stars are in their picture. Ask questions such as: "How many more planets are there than stars?"

○ Prepare a large weather chart as shown. Children can record the daily weather by pasting appropriate manipulatives (see page 50) on the chart. After four weeks, tally and graph to find how many sunny, rainy, windy, and cloudy days there were.

DAY	WEATHER
Monday	☀
Tuesday	☁
Wednesday	☁
Thursday	☀
Friday	☀

○ Ideas for using these manipulatives with story mats are provided in the Story Mats unit (see pages 61-72).

Weather

sun

rain

wind

clouds

snow

Weather

snowflakes

snowflakes

snowflakes

summer

winter

spring

fall

Space

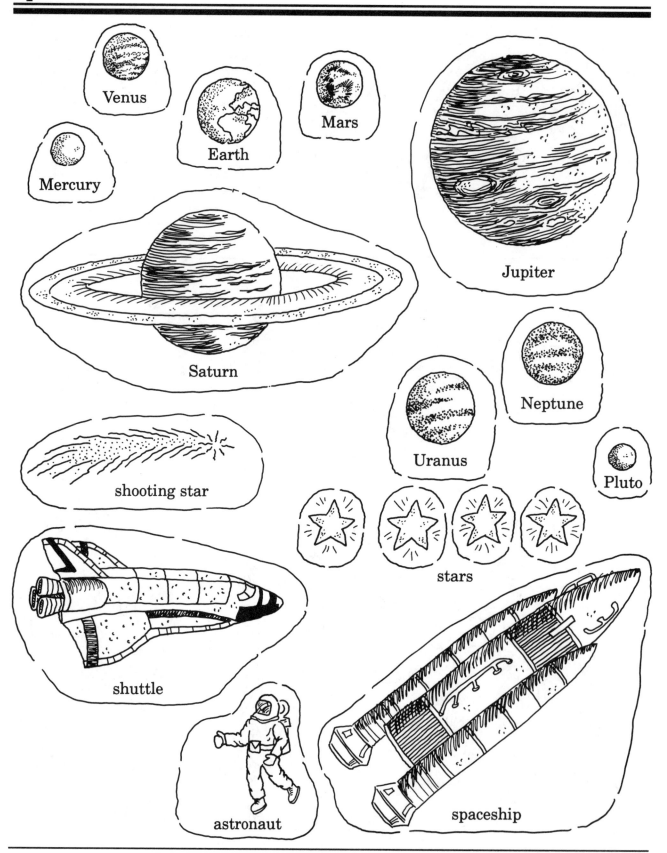

Venus

Earth

Mars

Mercury

Jupiter

Saturn

Neptune

Uranus

Pluto

shooting star

stars

shuttle

astronaut

spaceship

Seasons and Celebrations

Here are some suggestions for using the manipulatives in this unit:

○ For a springboard to Columbus Day activities, children can place manipulatives (see page 54) on blue paper, count the boats that Christopher Columbus used on his expedition, and arrange them from smallest to biggest. Practice ordinal positions by asking children which boat is first, second, and so on.

○ Display number cards from 1 to 9 (see page 89) as children display the corresponding number of candles in their menorahs (see page 56). As you proceed, ask questions such as "How many candles have we placed in the menorah?" "How many are left?" "How many more days of Hanukkah are there?" How can you tell?"

○ Copy the tree and ornaments (see page 57) onto transparencies. Invite children to take turns making matches with the ornaments and hanging them on the tree. Give children their own copies of the page and have them color the ornaments in pairs (for example, two with alternating red and green stripes, two with blue dots, and so on). Have children exchange ornaments to practice matching and creating patterns.

○ In celebration of Presidents' Day, give children a flag pattern (see page 59). Challenge them to estimate how many stars and stripes there are, then count them to see if they are right. When they are finished, invite them to color the flags and attach them to sticks or dowels for a parade.

○ For birthday celebrations any time of the year, pairs of children can take turns displaying number cards and the corresponding number of candles on the cake (see page 60). Next, give children cake and candle cutouts and ask them to arrange candles to show how old they will be on their next birthday. Make hats for "birthday children" to wear by pasting the appropriate number of candles to the rim of a paper crown.

○ Ideas for using these manipulatives with story mats are provided in the Story Mats unit (see pages 61-72).

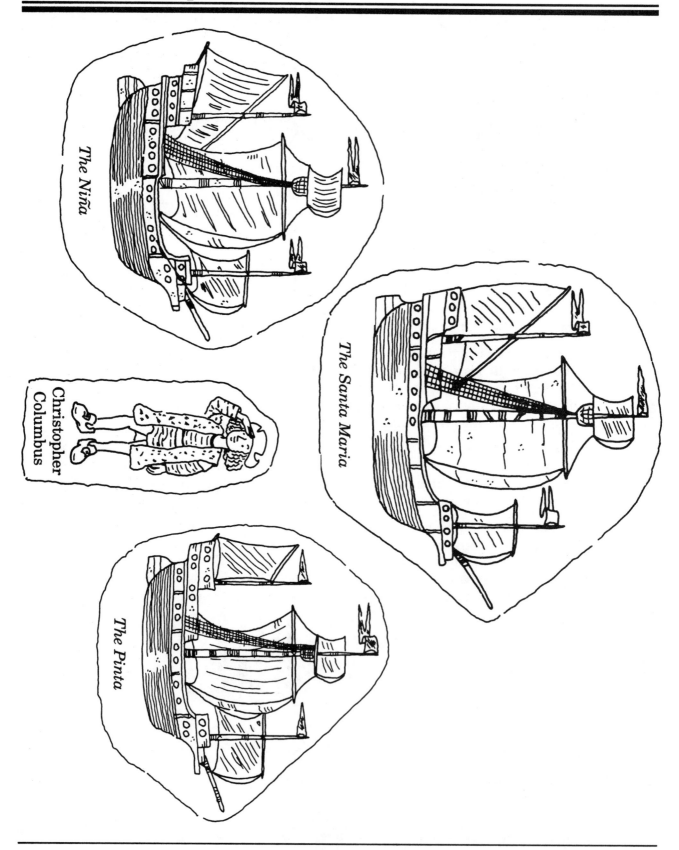

The Niña

The Santa Maria

The Pinta

Christopher Columbus

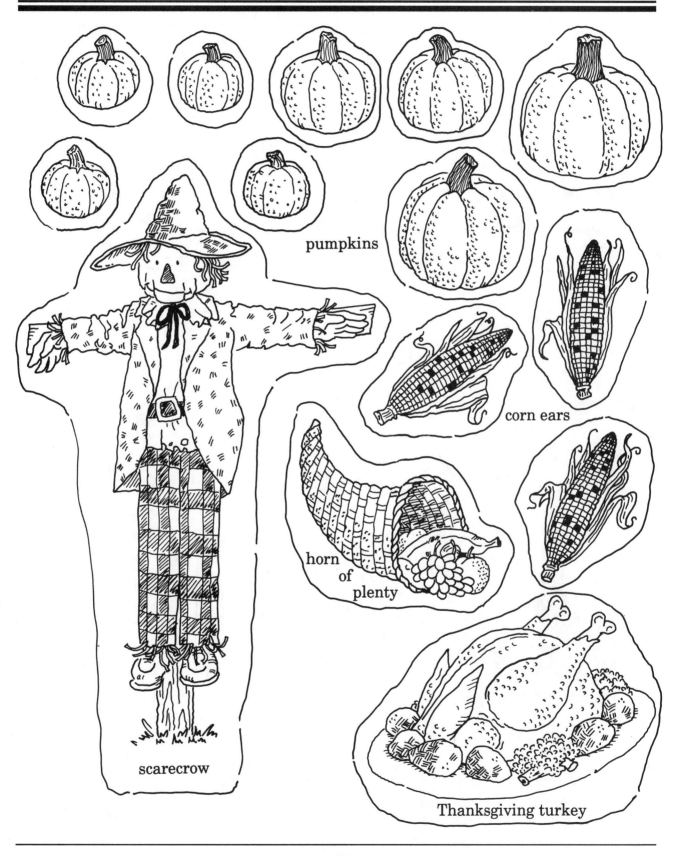

pumpkins

corn ears

horn of plenty

scarecrow

Thanksgiving turkey

Hanukkah

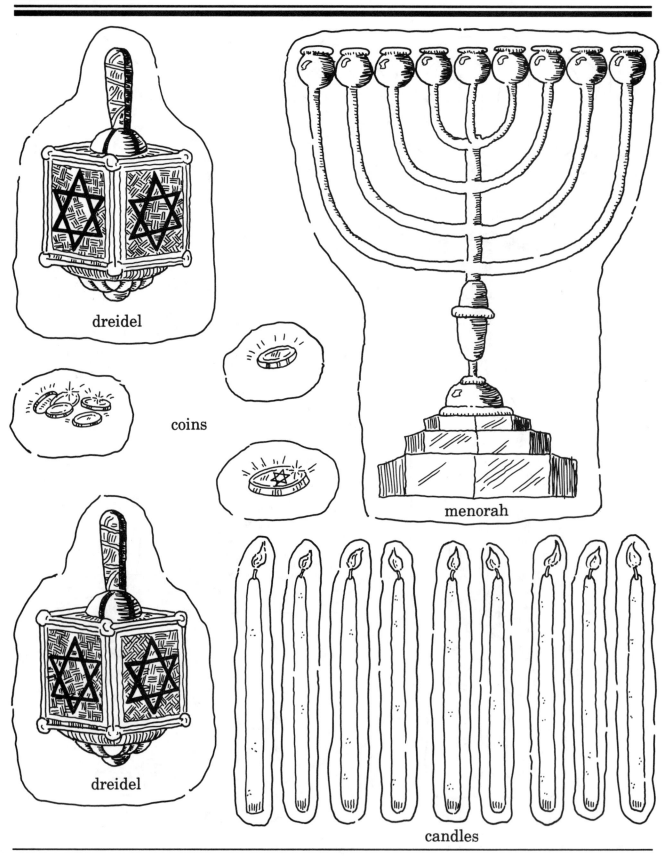

dreidel

coins

menorah

dreidel

candles

Christmas

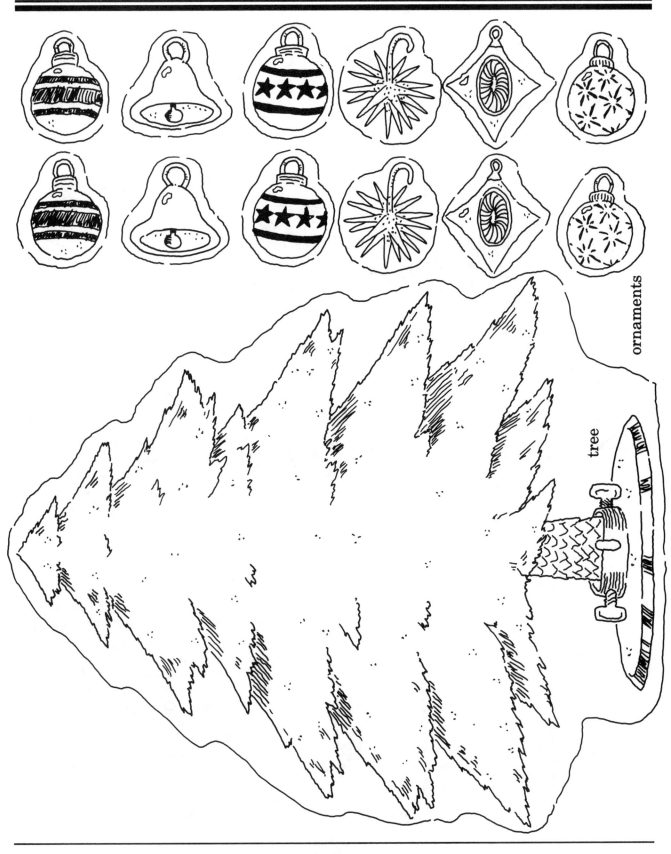

ornaments

tree

Chinese dragon

piñata

hearts

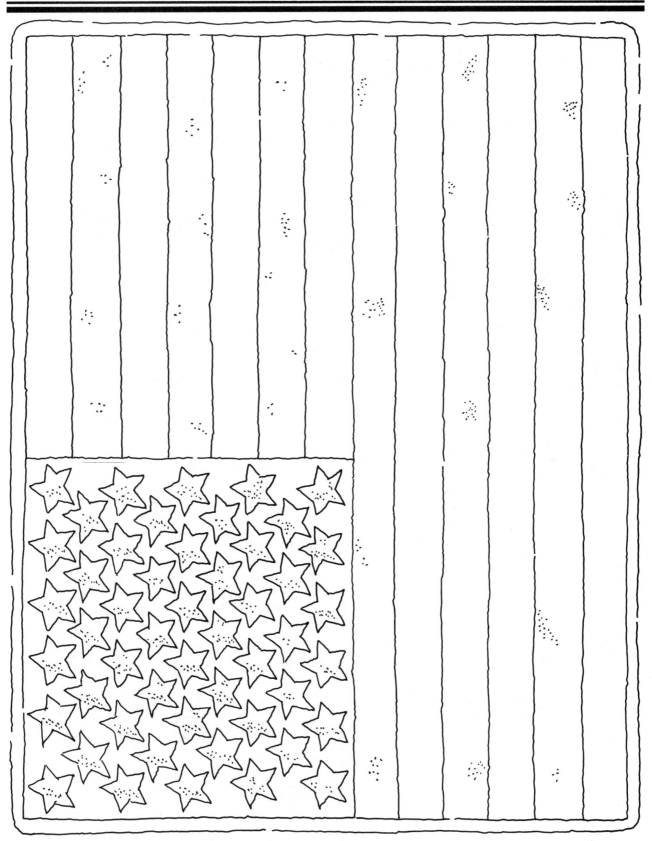

candles

cake

Story Mats

Children can combine manipulatives from any of the previous units with the story mats in this unit to create pictures and solve problems at the same time. Choose from a farm, a meadow, a beach, outer space, a garden, a city, a jungle, and a toy room. A sorting mat and a graphing mat expand the learning opportunities and, like the story mats, can be used over and over with many of the suggestions in the book or to enhance your existing program. Children may enjoy pasting story mats on the inside of boxes to create dioramas. Children can tell number stories about dioramas created by classmates.

Other suggestions for using story mats include:

Sorting Mat (see page 63):

Children can sort and classify any of the manipulatives in this section on the sorting mat. Provide two mats for children to let them experiment with sorting into more than two groups. Some of the many ways children can sort are by:
   O objects that are longer or shorter than a given object;
   O animals that swim, fly, crawl, hop, or run;
   O shapes (leaves, shells);
   O size (small or large);
   O vehicles with wheels or vehicles without wheels.

Farm or Meadow Story Mat (see pages 64-65):

Children can paste cutouts in each scene, then write number stories about their pictures. Number stories can be shared with the class or stapled together into a book for children to solve at a later time.

For example:

O Tulips, daisies, and dandelions are growing in a meadow. There are 3 tulips, 4 more dandelions than tulips, and 2 fewer daisies than dandelions. How many of each kind of flower is growing by the pond? (3 tulips, 7 dandelions, 5 daisies)

O Carla's job on the farm is to feed the baby animals. One morning she fed 3 chicks and 4 ducklings. How many animals did she feed? (7)

O A turkey, a goat, a pig, and a goose all went to get a drink. The goat took a drink first. The goose took a drink last. The pig took a drink after the turkey. In what order did the animals take their drinks? (goat, turkey, pig, goose)

Children can model addition and subtraction stories as they move animal manipulatives in and out of the barn or pond.

continued

Story Mats *continued*

To compare sets, have children model stories such as: "There are 8 frogs in the pond. There are fewer rabbits in the meadow. How many rabbits could be in the meadow? Show me."

Beach, Garden, or Jungle Story Mat (see pages 66, 68, 70):

Children can use animals, insects, natural objects, or people with these story mats. Give small groups of children number cards (see pages 89-90). One child draws two number cards. A second child places manipulatives on the story mats to model the numbers. A third child tells a story about the manipulatives.

Pairs of children can paste manipulatives in place on a story mat to design a setting, then count and make a graph to show how many of each type of manipulative was used.

Children can create story problems using the animal cutouts and jungle story mat, such as:

○ Six hungry tigers are looking for food together in a jungle. Three tigers wandered off to the water. How many tigers are still together looking for food? (3)

Using beach manipulatives, children can depict solutions to story problems, such as:

○ Marc found 2 clam shells, 6 oyster shells, and 4 cockleshells. How many shells did Marc find? (12) Marc is making a pattern with the shells he finds. He arranges them like this:

What would come next in Marc's pattern? What shell will Marc run out of first? Second? (clam; cockleshell)

Space, City, and Toy Room Story Mat (see pages 67, 69, 71):

Using large and small buildings on the city story mat, children can create patterned streets. Follow up by asking children to describe patterns on the streets where they live.

Children can arrange toys in the toy room using positional terms such as top, middle, bottom, above, below, inside, outside, and so on. Then look around the classroom at toys (or other materials). Ask questions such as "What is above the box of blocks? Next to it?"

Place a copy of the space story mat in a math center. Cut out and laminate space manipulatives to use on the story mat. Children can take turns placing quantities of stars in space while a friend estimates how many stars there are, then counts to check.

Graphing Mat (see page 72):

Children can visually record data they collect in various activities suggested throughout the book. Cut off one column if a two-column graph is needed, or paste copies together if four or more columns are needed. Use manipulatives to make picture graphs, pasting on objects that correspond to information children gather. Students might ask, for example, "Do you prefer milk or juice?" then use the manipulatives on page 72 to graph survey results.

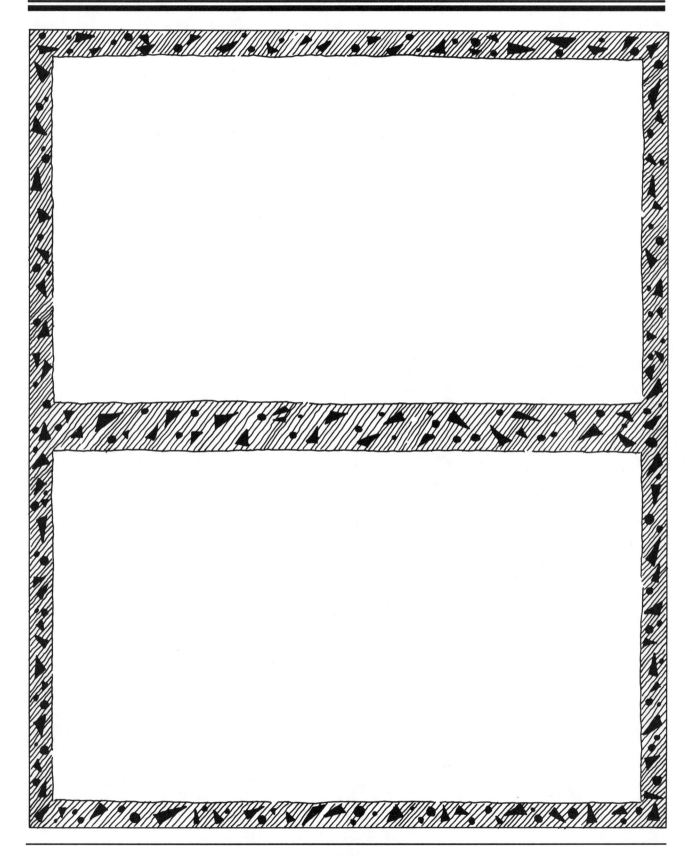

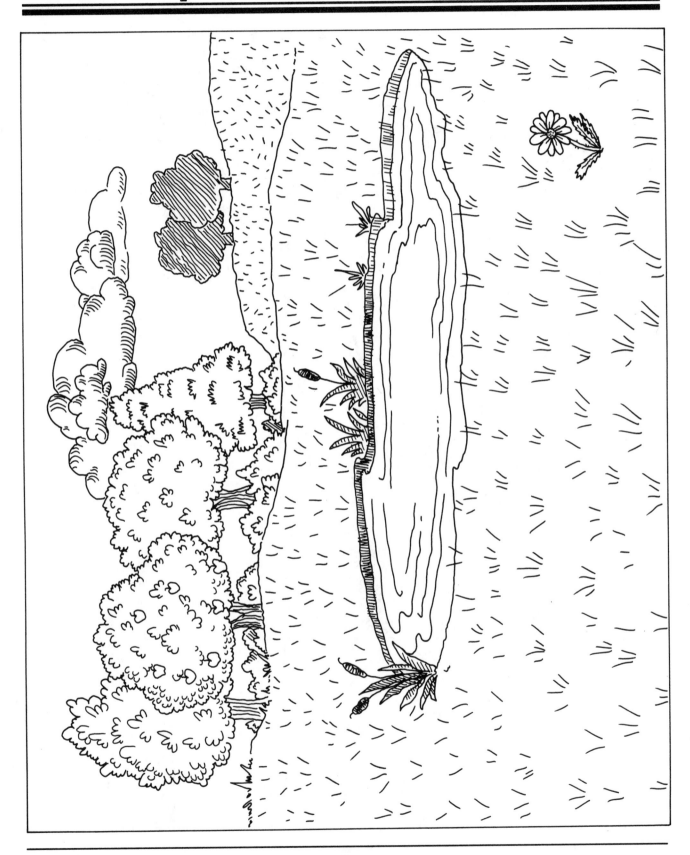

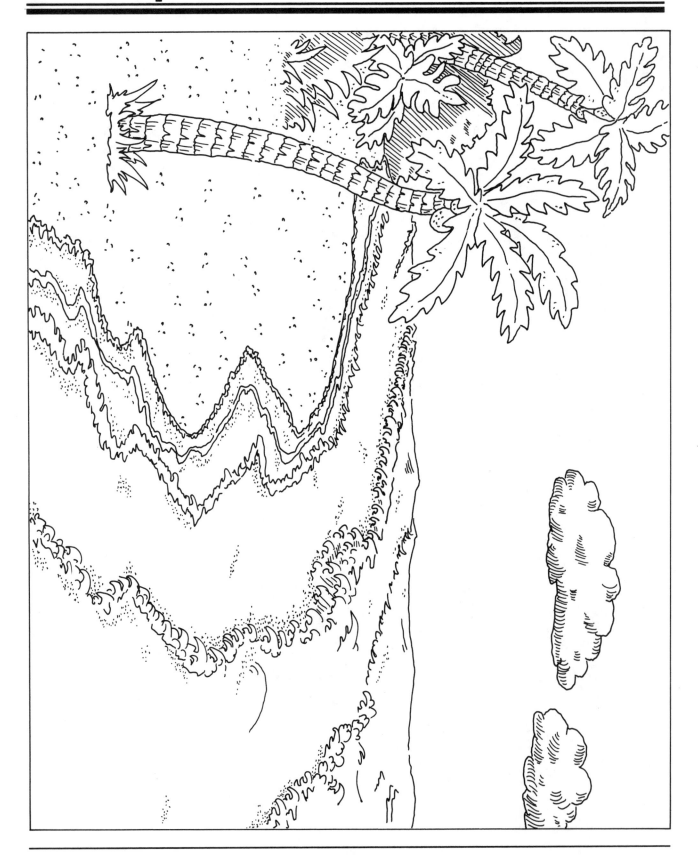

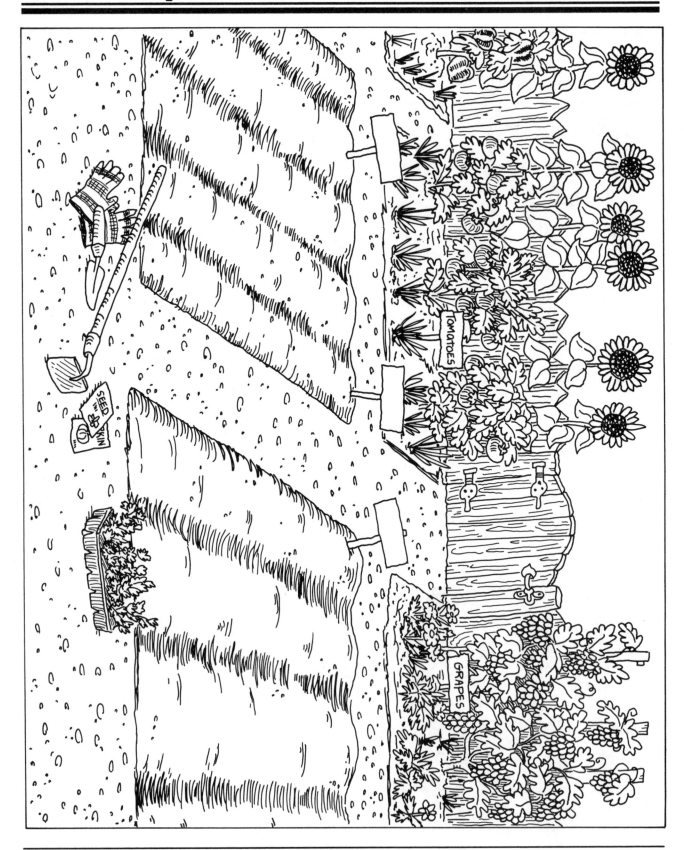

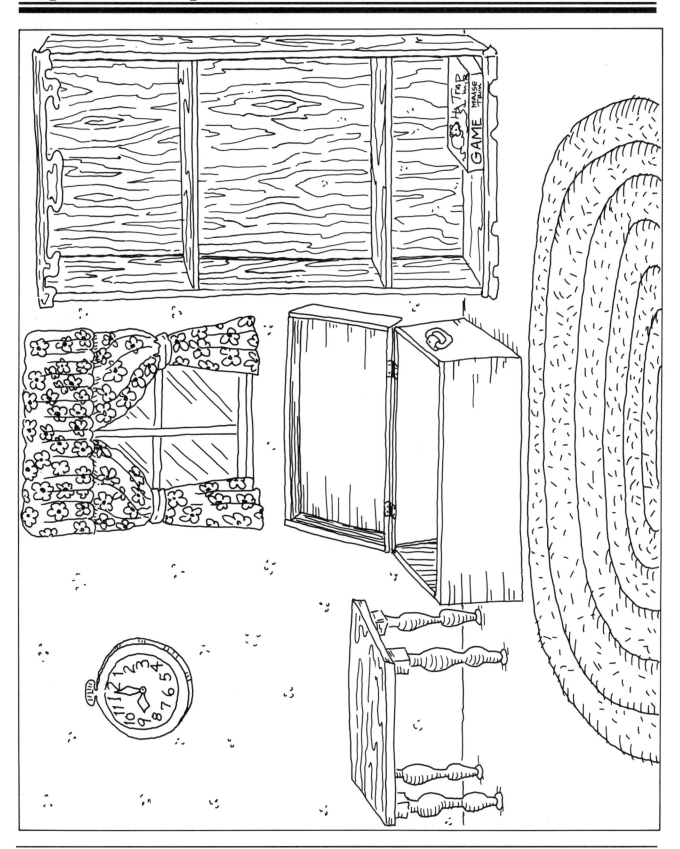

Graphing Mat

section 2

Patterns and Relationships

Here are some suggestions for using the manipulatives and reproducibles in this unit:

○ **Pattern and Shape Discovery Page (see page 75):** Prepare quantities of this page for children to record observations as they work with attribute and shape manipulatives. As children complete several of these record sheets, they'll enjoy comparing their first observations to later discoveries. For example, at first, children may simply see a circular shape represented by a clock. As they become more familiar with the shape manipulatives and their surroundings, they may begin to notice shapes within shapes. A pencil's eraser is like the circle, the tip is like the triangle.

○ **Attribute Buttons, Attribute Shapes, Attribute Cards (see pages 76-78):** Provide each child with four copies of Attribute Buttons and three copies of Attribute Shapes. Children can color and cut as indicated and store each set in a labeled envelope. Children can sort by attributes such as color, shape, or size, using the Attribute Cards.

○ **Pattern Shapes (see pages 79-80):** Children can color and cut apart the shapes, then create patterns with color, shape, and position patterns or designs. As they explore, children may notice relationships among the pieces, for example: 1 hexagon = 2 trapezoids, 3 parallelograms, or 6 triangles.

○ **Tangram (see pages 81-82):** These puzzle pieces can be used to form an unending variety of figures and shapes. After children form some basic shapes as indicated, encourage them to form recognizable figures of their own, then paste the pieces on paper to make a recording. Children can carefully trace over the figures, make outlines of the shapes, and create a class tangram puzzle book for others to try.

○ **Pentominoes (see pages 83-84):** Each pentomino piece resembles a letter, as shown:

F   I   L   N   P   T   U   V   W   X   Y   Z

Children can use these pieces to form many shapes and figures. A few examples are shown. As with the tangrams, have children outline pentomino shapes they create and challenge their classmates to find the pieces that fit. Is there ever more than one solution?

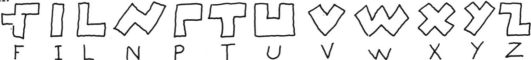

Pattern and Shape Discovery Page

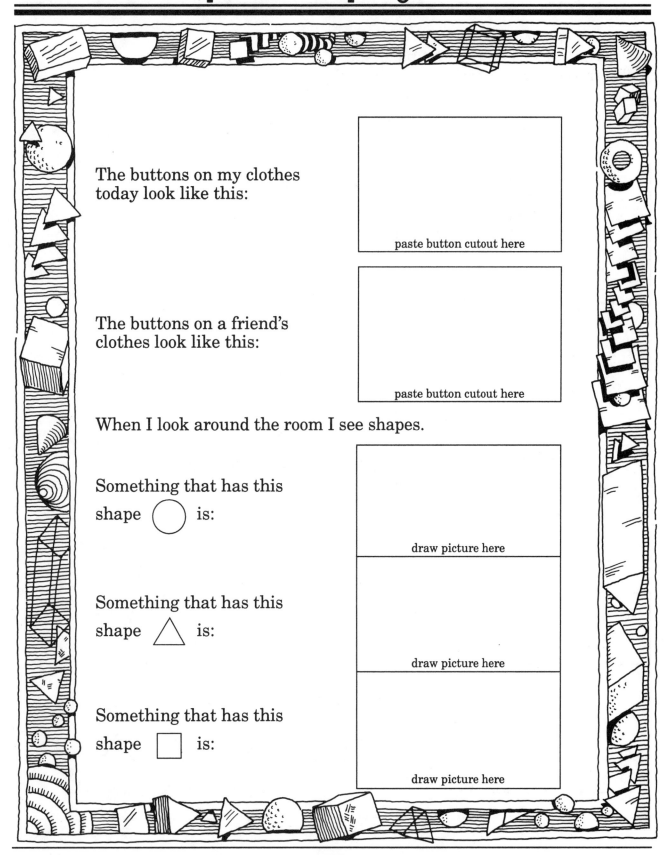

The buttons on my clothes today look like this:

paste button cutout here

The buttons on a friend's clothes look like this:

paste button cutout here

When I look around the room I see shapes.

Something that has this shape ◯ is:

draw picture here

Something that has this shape △ is:

draw picture here

Something that has this shape ▢ is:

draw picture here

Attribute Buttons

(Teacher: Make four copies for each set.)
Color the buttons on the first page red.
Color the buttons on the second page yellow.
Color the buttons on the third page blue.
Color the buttons on the fourth page green.

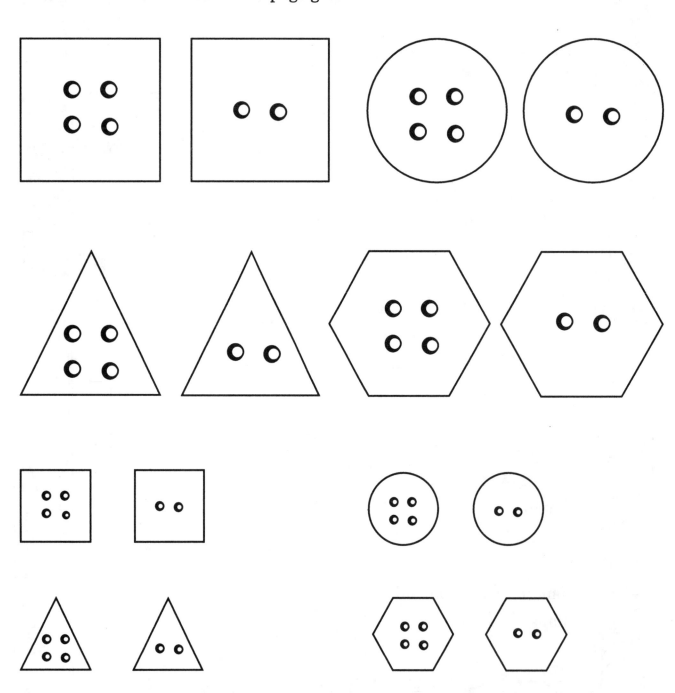

Attribute Shapes

(Teacher: Make three copies for each set.)
Color the blocks on the first page red.
Color the blocks on the second page blue.
Color the blocks on the third page yellow.

Attribute Cards

Cut apart the cards.
Use the cards to sort shapes and buttons.

small	not small	large
not large	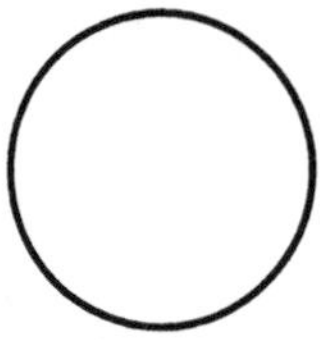	
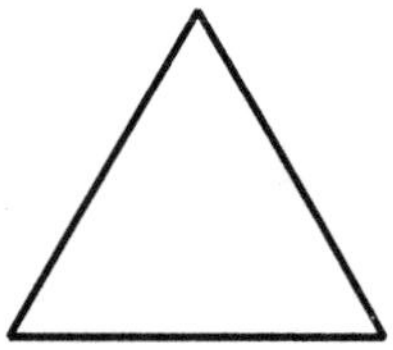	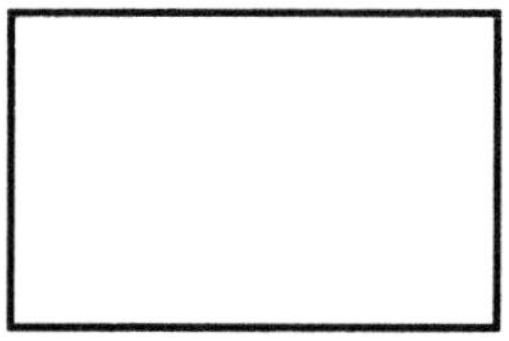	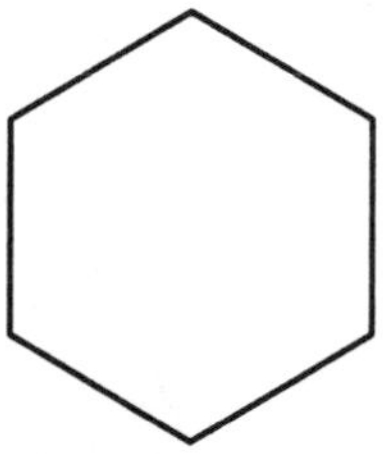
red	not red	yellow
not yellow	blue	not blue

Pattern Shapes

Color the ⬡ yellow.

Color the ⏢ red.

Color the ▱ blue.

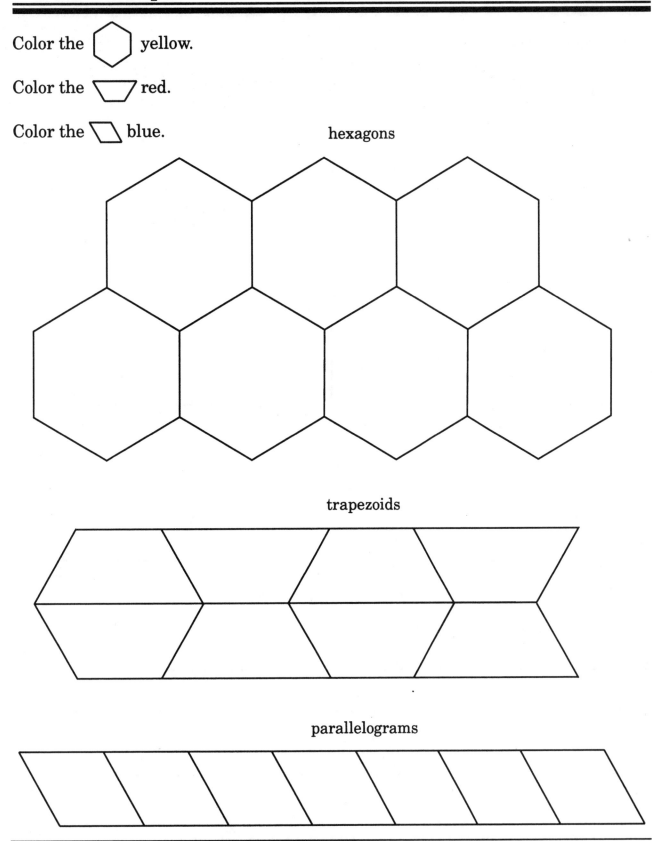

hexagons

trapezoids

parallelograms

Pattern Shapes

Color the ☐ orange.

Color the △ green.

Color the ▱ yellow.

squares

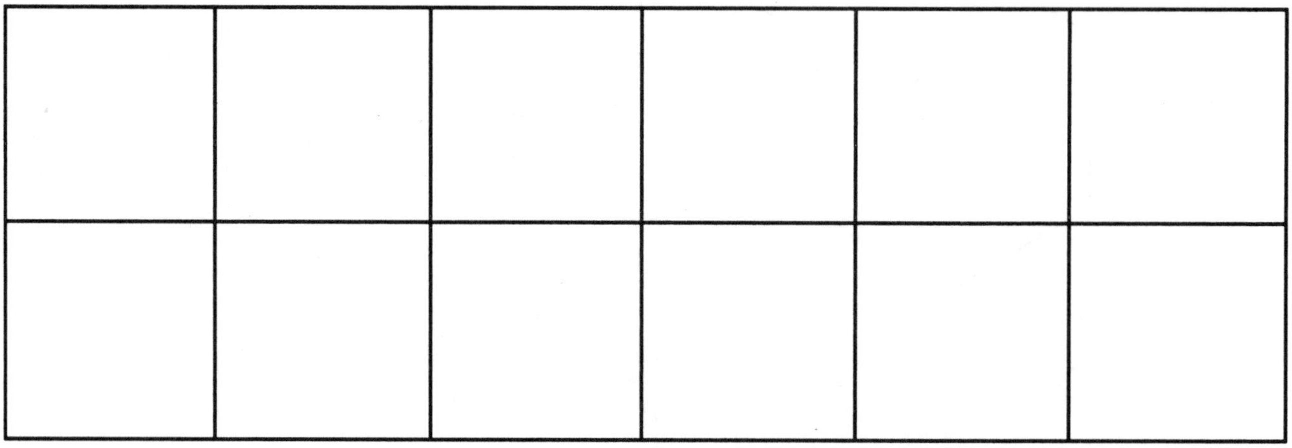

triangles

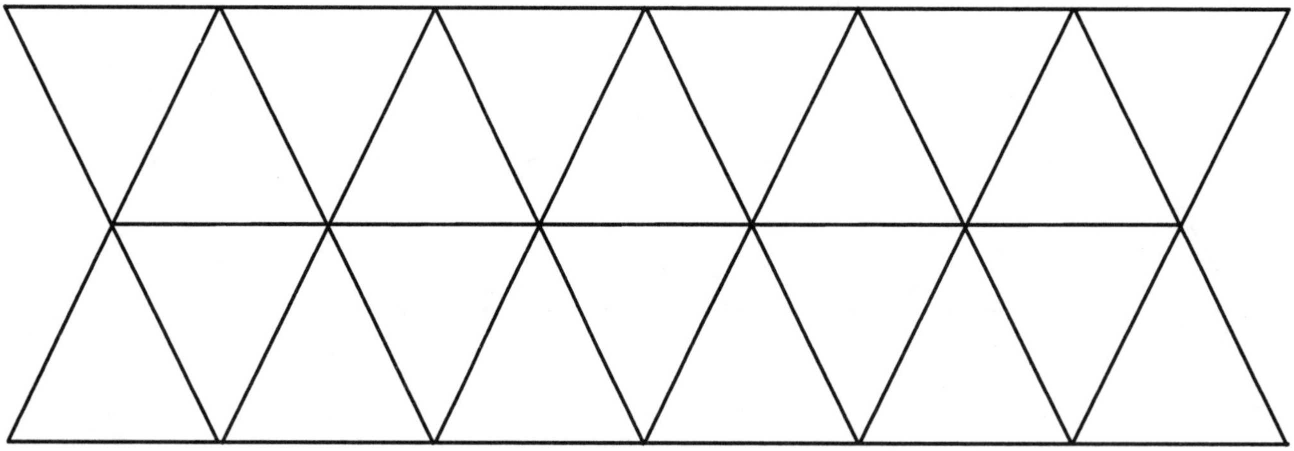

rhombuses

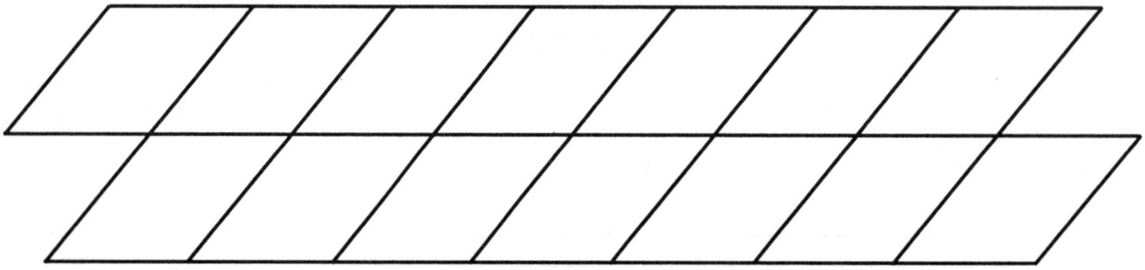

Pentominoes

Cut out the pentomino shapes.
Put the shapes together to form other shapes.

Pentominoes

Cut out the pentomino shapes.
Put the shapes together to form other shapes.

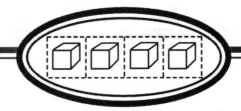

Place Value Materials

Here are some suggestions for using the manipulatives and reproducibles in this unit:

○ **Place Value Models and Place Value Chart (see pages 86-88):** Using the place value models and place value chart, let children arrange models on the chart, then show corresponding number cards (see pages 89-90).

○ **Blank Number Lines (see page 92):** Paste two copies of the number lines together to form a number line from 1 to 100. Use the number line in estimation activities. For example, ask "How many Mondays are there in 100 days of school?" Have children record their guesses. Select a different color for each day of the week (Monday, green; Tuesday, red, and so on), then color in a space on the number line each day. As children begin to get a better sense of how many green squares there are "so far" (for example, they might see that the paper is almost half colored in, count 7 green squares, and realize that a guess of 5 is too low and 20 is too high), encourage them to revise their estimates.

○ **Hundreds Chart (See page 91):** Partners can take turns using beans or cubes to cover the counting patterns on the hundreds chart as they skip count by 2, 3, 5, 10, and so on. Once they have completed the count, children can make records by coloring the patterns on copies of the chart. Keep copies of the hundreds chart available for children. Let them look for as many patterns as they can find, then color to record their observations. Other activities include: adding or subtracting one- and two-digit numbers on the hundreds chart. Show children these moves:

```
 1  2  3  4  5  6  7  8  9 10
11 12 13 14 15 16 17 18 19 20
21 22 23 24 25 26 27 28 29 30
31 32 33 34 35 36 37 38 39 40
41 42 43 44 45 46 47 48 49 50
```

To find the sum of 14 and 25, begin at 14, move down two rows to add 2 tens, then move right five spaces to add 5 ones. The sum is 39.

Similarly, to find the difference between 72 and 34, begin at 72, move up three rows to 42 (subtracting 3 tens) and to the left four spaces (subtracting 4 ones). To continue the move left, you must move up one row and all the way to the right (to 40) as you count backwards. The difference is 38. Children can take turns plotting moves on the chart to represent equations for classmates to "calculate."

○ Children can cut the hundred chart along the lines (using combinations of horizontal, vertical, and diagonal cuts) to make puzzle pieces. Pairs of children can solve each other's puzzles.

Place Value Models: Ones and Tens

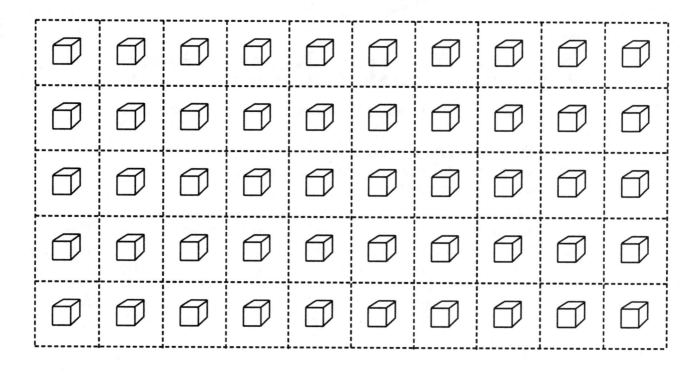

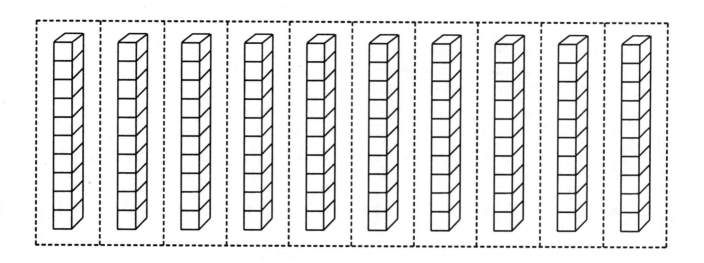

Place Value Models: Tens and Hundreds

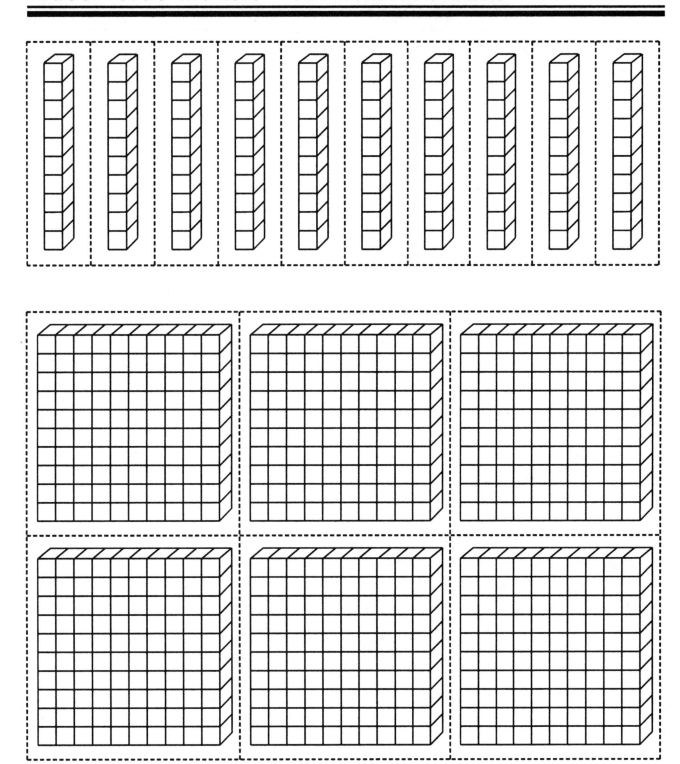

Place Value Chart

hundreds	tens	ones

Number Cards

0	1	2	3
4	5	6	7
8	9	10	11
12	13	14	15
16	17	18	19

20	21	22	23
24	25	26	27
28	29	30	+
-	×	÷	=
>	>	<	<

Hundreds Chart

1	2	3	4	5	6	7	8	9	10
11	12	13	14	15	16	17	18	19	20
21	22	23	24	25	26	27	28	29	30
31	32	33	34	35	36	37	38	39	40
41	42	43	44	45	46	47	48	49	50
51	52	53	54	55	56	57	58	59	60
61	62	63	64	65	66	67	68	69	70
71	72	73	74	75	76	77	78	79	80
81	82	83	84	85	86	87	88	89	90
91	92	93	94	95	98	97	98	99	100

Blank Number Lines

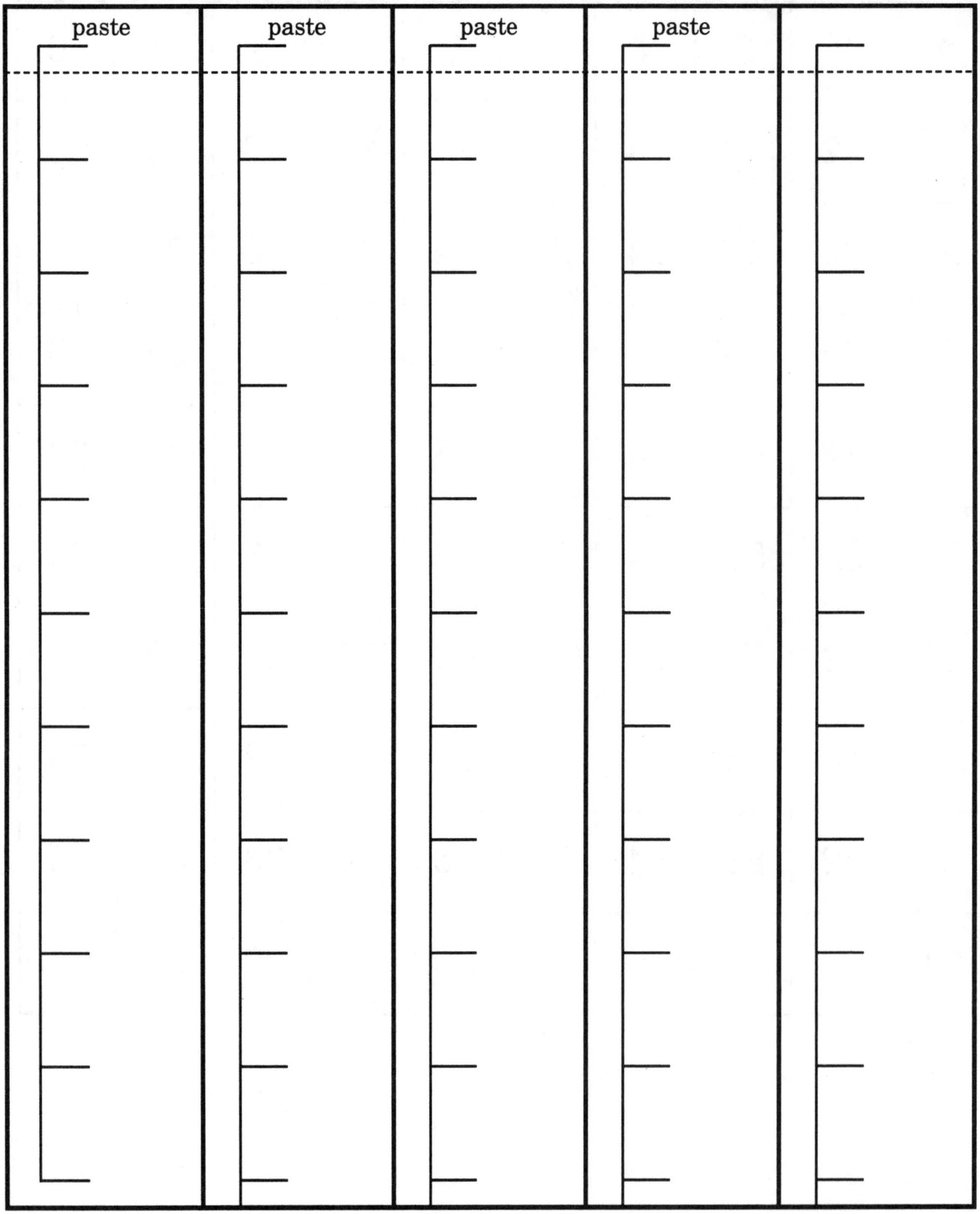

paste	paste	paste	paste	

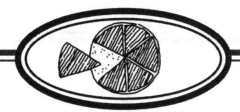

Geometry and Fractions

Here are some suggestions for using the manipulatives in this unit:

○ **Cube, Rectangular Prism, Cylinder, and Cone Patterns (see pages 94-97):** Children can cut apart, fold, and tape together the patterns to form cubes, rectangular prisms, cylinders, and cones. Encourage them to experiment with these figures to see which will slide and/or roll.

○ **Objects All Around (see page 98):** After children cut apart the objects, they can sort by shape, purpose, or size. Challenge children match the object cutouts to real objects in the classroom that have the same shape or size.

○ **Circles, Squares, Triangles, Rectangles (see page 99):** Children can cut apart the shapes, talk about the number of sides and corners they see, form patterns and designs, and match shapes to find circles, squares, and triangles that are congruent (same size and shape).

○ **Circle Fractions (see page 100):** To play a fraction game, give pairs of children 6 whole circles (three per child), and fractional parts for halves, thirds, fourths, and sixths. In turn, players draw one fractional part and place it on a whole shape. The first child to form two whole circles wins.

○ **Rectangle Fractions (see page 101):** Copy the rectangular parts onto construction paper and attach felt strips to the back of the halves, thirds, fourths, sixths, and eights. Work with small groups of children at the flannel board to find equivalent parts such as one-third and two-sixths, one-half and two-fourths, and so on.

Cube Pattern

Cut along the solid line.
Fold along the dashed lines.

Tape together to form a 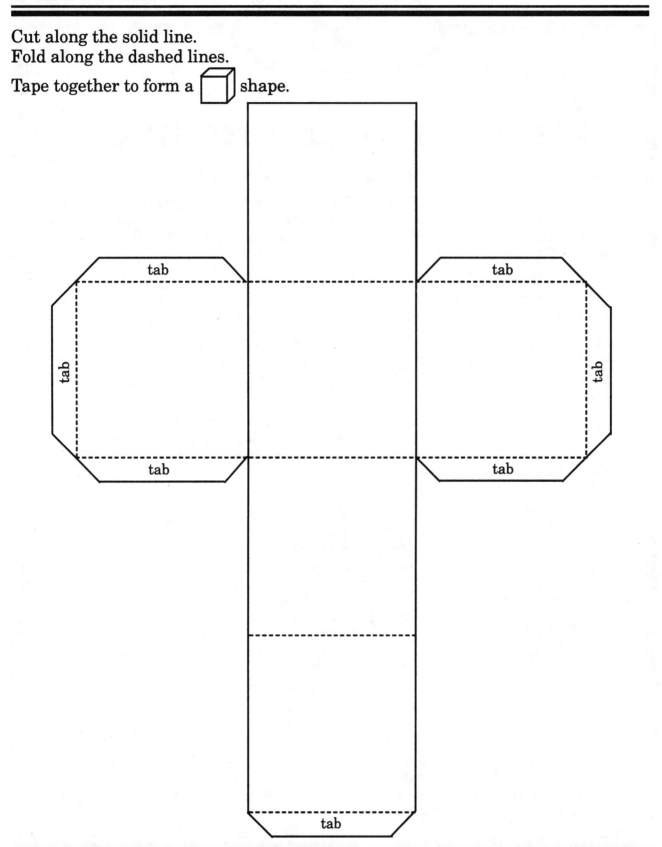 shape.

Rectangular Prism Pattern

Cut out along the solid line.
Fold along the dashed lines.
Tape together to form a

shape.

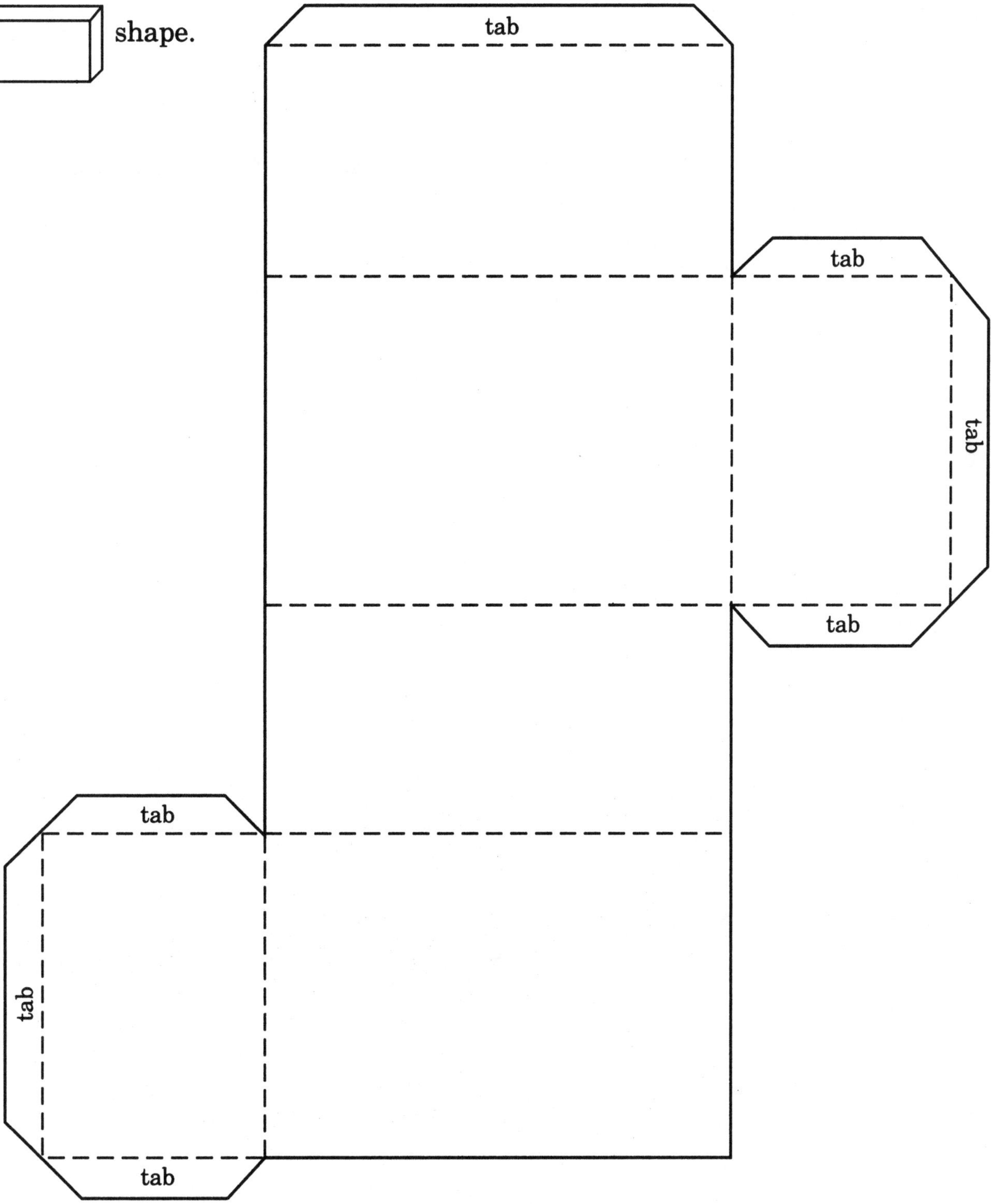

tab

tab

tab

tab

tab

tab

tab

Cylinder Pattern

Cut out along the solid line.
Fold along the dashed lines.

Tape together to form a 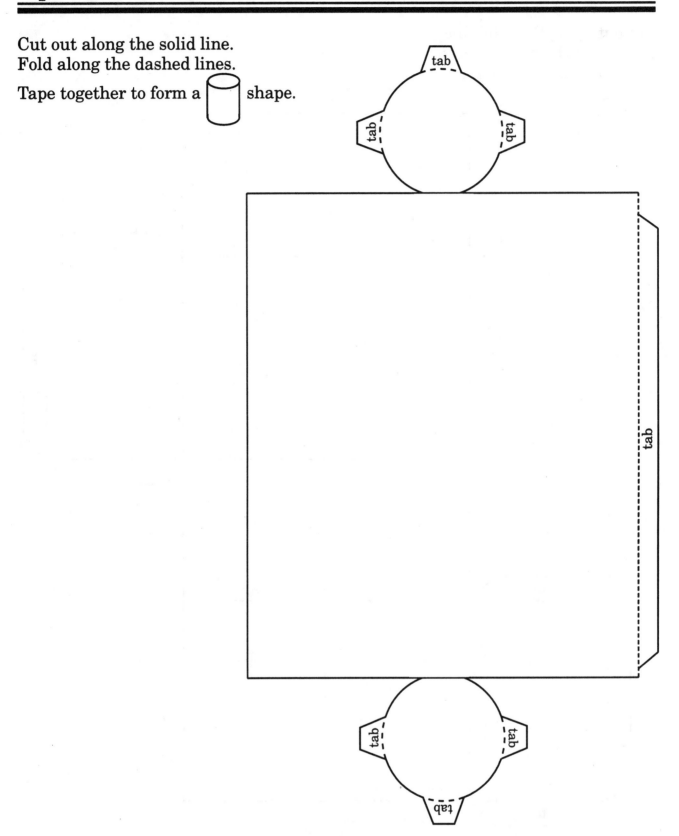 shape.

Cone Pattern

Cut out along the solid line.
Fold along the dashed lines.
Tape together to form a

 shape.

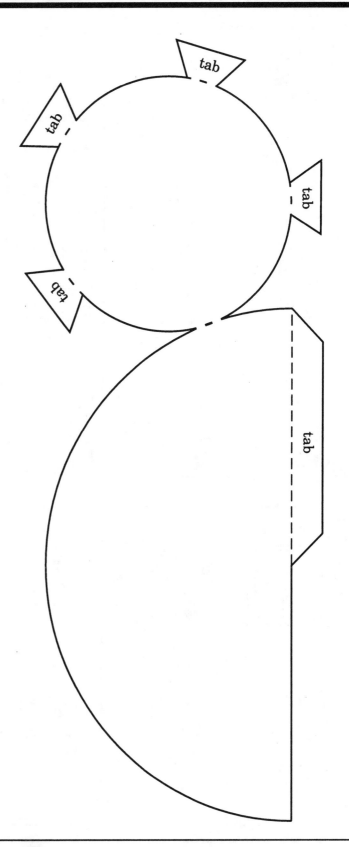

Circles, Squares, Triangles, Rectangles

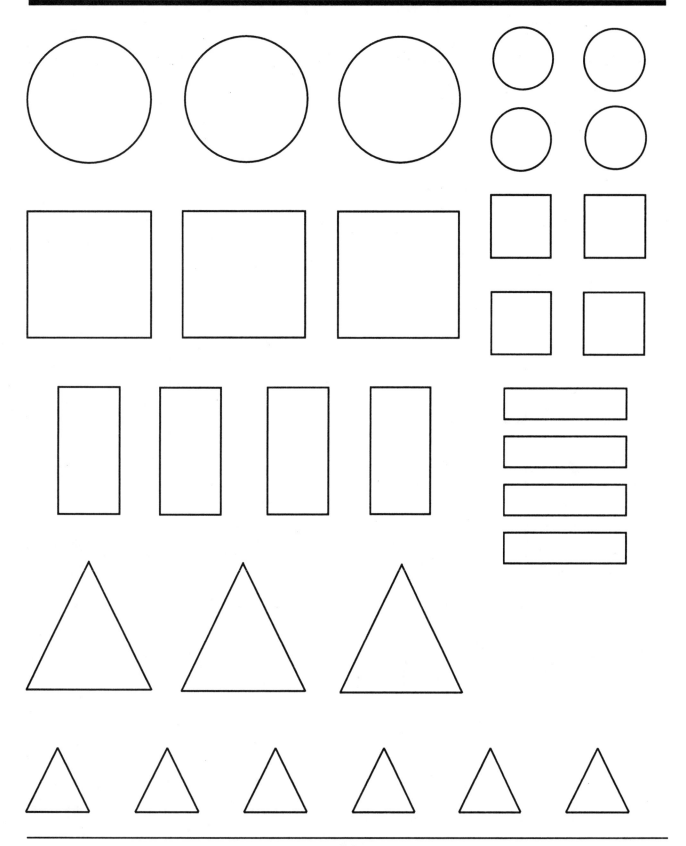

Fractions: Circles

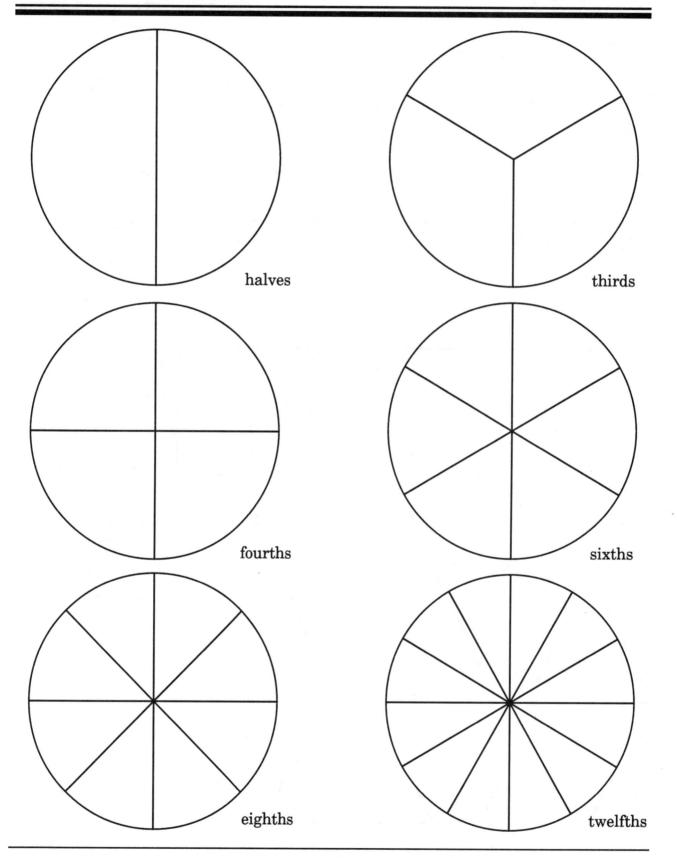

halves

thirds

fourths

sixths

eighths

twelfths

Fractions: Rectangles

halves

thirds

fourths

sixths

eighths

twelfths

Measurement

Here are some suggestions for using the manipulatives and reproducibles in this unit:

○ **Inch/Yard Rulers and Centimeter/Meter Stick (see pages 103-104):** Children can cut apart and paste together the standard and metric measures, then paste a yard (meter) stick on paper. Attach the paper to the wall 24 inches above the ground. Use this for estimating and measuring children's height. After measuring one child, invite children to use that information to estimate their own height. Are they taller, shorter, or about the same? Have children estimate then measure to check. Children can compare their height in inches and centimeters.

○ **Thermometers (see page 105):** Children can record the temperature over the course of a day, for several days, or once a week for several weeks and graph as they go to record and compare findings.

○ **Graph Paper (see pages 106-107):** Color to record linear patterns or make graphs to record surveys and other information.

○ **Dot Paper (see page 108):** Children can use dot paper to explore congruent and similar figures, and figures with lines of symmetry.

Introduce the concept of congruence by drawing a simple shape, such as a triangle, on dot paper. Draw a similar shape on the same paper that is not quite the same size and one that is the same size and shape. Ask children how the figures are alike. Encourage them to move toward realizing that two of the figures are the same size and shape. How can they tell? Invite children to show how they can make figures that are the same size and shape on their dot paper. Challenge children to identify congruent shapes in the classroom (the ends or sides of a box, the top and bottom of a glue stick, and so on).

○ **Analog and Digital Clocks (see pages 109-110):** Assemble the analog clock with a paper fastener. The digital clock can be assembled by placing the two strips in each part of the clock to show hours and minutes. Children can cut apart the Time Pictures (see pages 111-112) and arrange them to show a sequence of events. Invite children to draw their own pictures (for example, about their day, an event, and so on), cut them apart, and ask classmates to sequence them.

○ **Items for Sale (see page 115):** Fill in the price tags on the top of the page with amounts that match the coin cards on the bottom of the page (50¢, 46¢, 85¢, 25¢, 8¢, 92¢). Have children play a matching game by pairing items with coin cards. Or, complete the price tags with other amounts and have children make their own matching coin cards by pasting coin cutouts on small cards.

Inch/Yard Ruler

Cut apart the ruler on the -------- lines.
Paste together the tabs to form a yardstick.

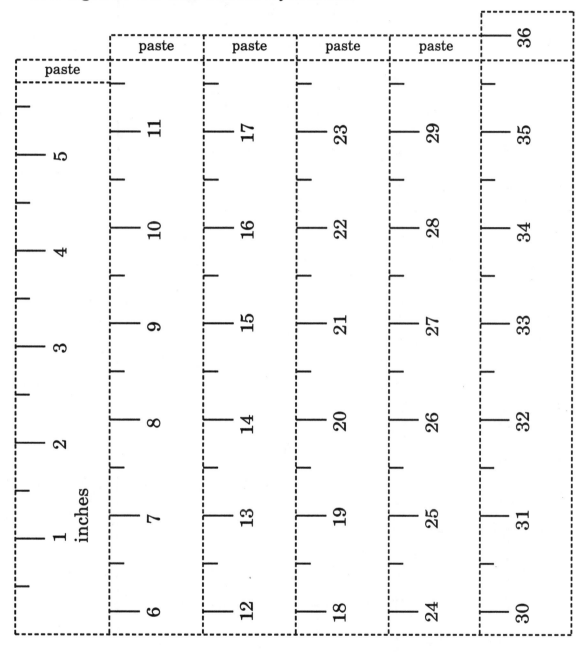

Centimeter/Meter Ruler

Cut apart the ruler on the -------- lines.
Paste together the tabs to form a meter measure.

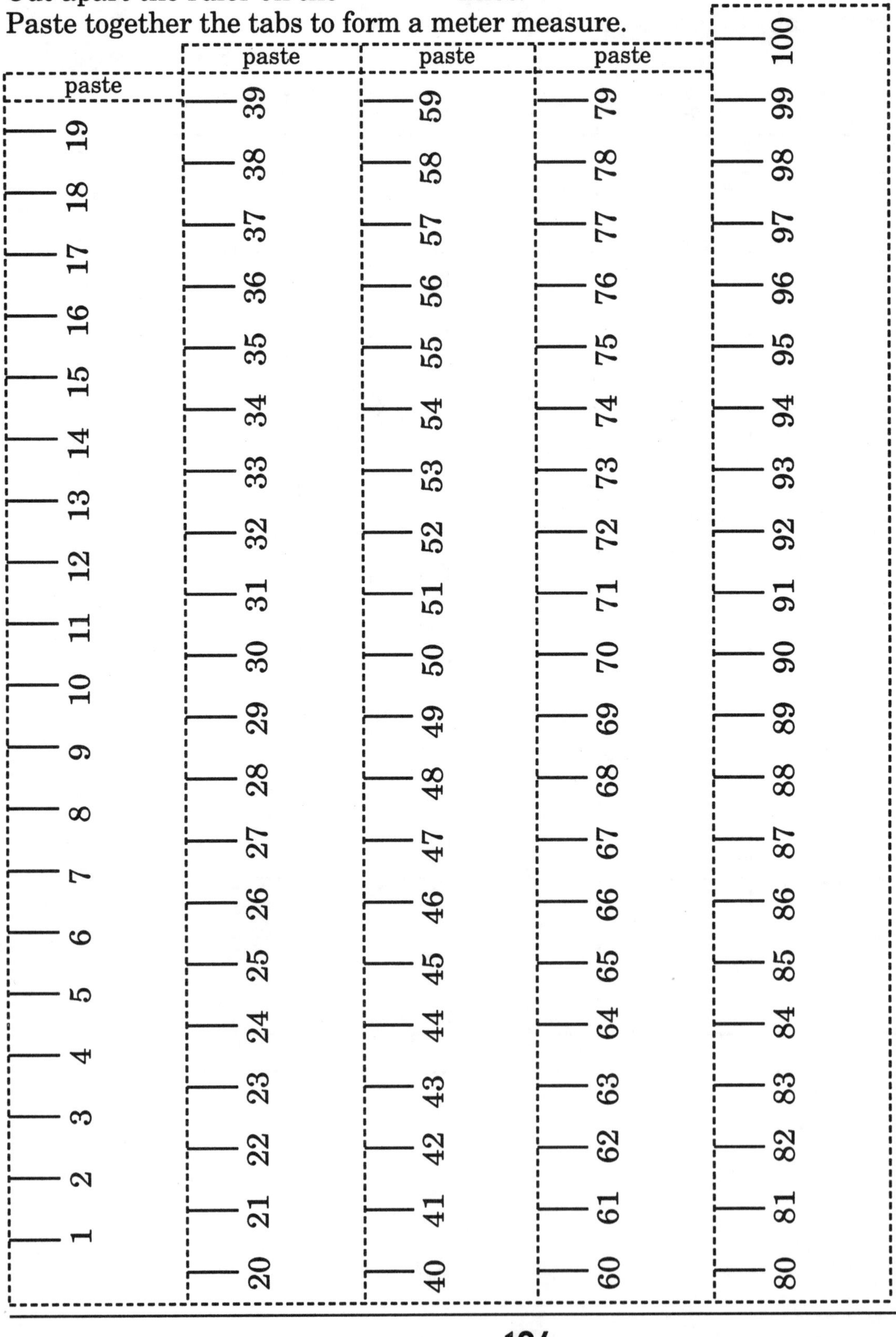
paste
paste
paste
paste
1 2 3 4 5 6 7 8 9 10 11 12 13 14 15 16 17 18 19
20 21 22 23 24 25 26 27 28 29 30 31 32 33 34 35 36 37 38 39
40 41 42 43 44 45 46 47 48 49 50 51 52 53 54 55 56 57 58 59
60 61 62 63 64 65 66 67 68 69 70 71 72 73 74 75 76 77 78 79
80 81 82 83 84 85 86 87 88 89 90 91 92 93 94 95 96 97 98 99 100

Thermometers °F and °C

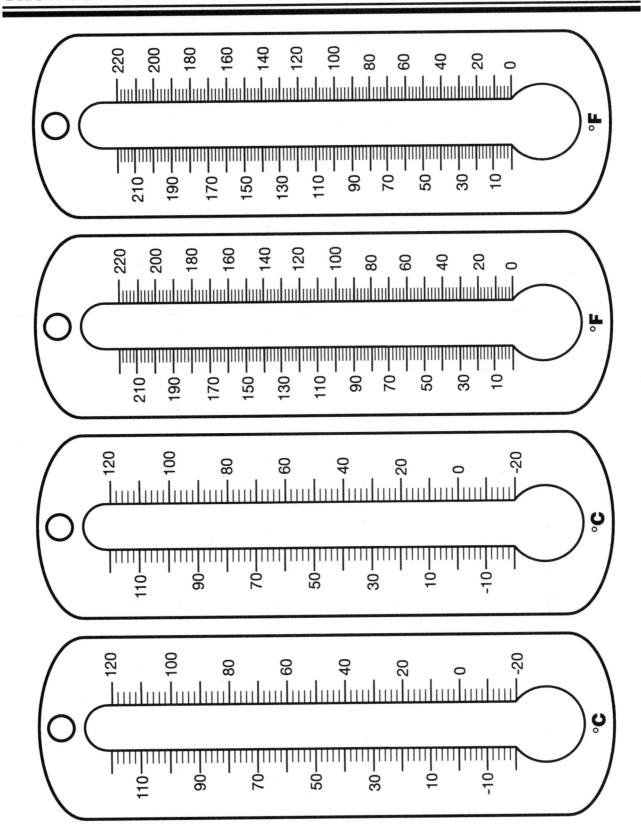

Inch Graph Paper

Centimeter Graph Paper

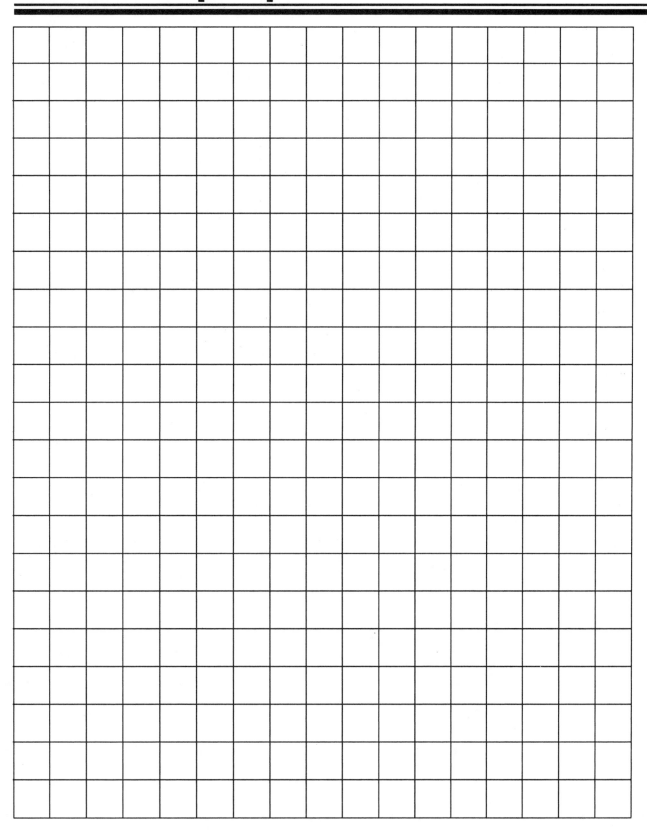

Dot Paper

Analog Clock

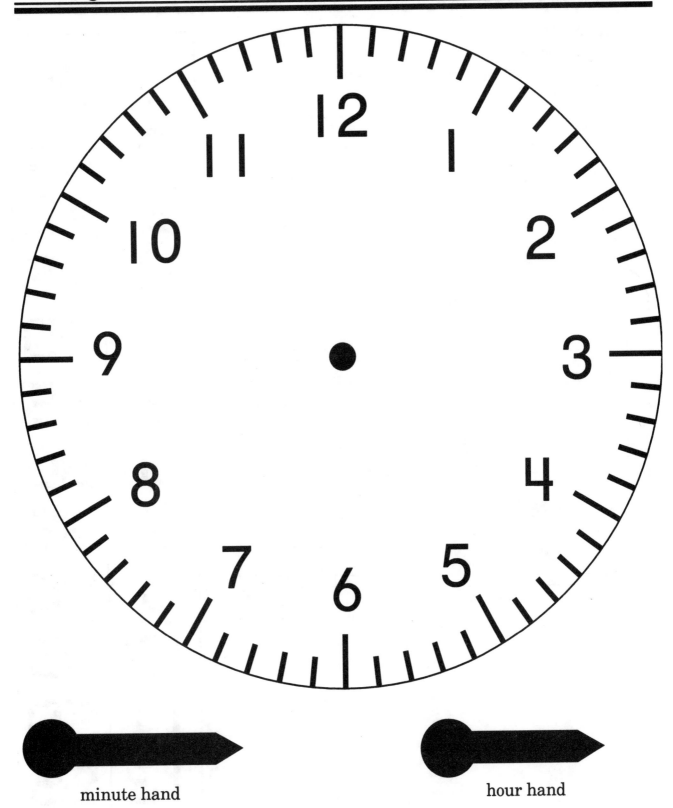

minute hand   hour hand

Digital Clock

Cut apart the clock.
Cut out the slits.
Insert a number strip in each of the slits.

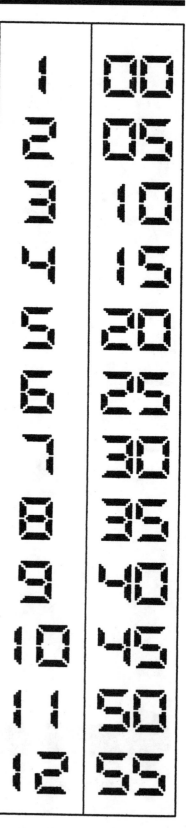

Time Pictures

Cut out the pictures.
Paste them in order to tell a story.

Time Pictures

Cut out the pictures.
Paste them in order to tell a story.

Coins

Bills

Items for Sale

Games

○ **Game Board 1 (see page 118):** Children can make number cubes (see page 121) or spinners (see page 120) and play a variety of simple games on this board. Younger children can roll one cube or spinner and count out that many spaces on the game board, continuing until one child reaches finish. Older children can roll both cubes or spinners, find the sum, then move the total number of spaces. Or, fold and tape the cubes so the numbers are on the inside. Draw circles, squares, triangles, and rectangles on each of the empty faces. Children can move ahead on the game board by matching the shapes.

○ **Game Board 2 (see page 119):** Children can use Game Board 2 to go shopping. Using the coins and bills (see pages 113-114), each child starts the game with money to go shopping. Price the items pictured on the game board then cut them out. Children can make purchases as they land on shopping squares along the game board. At the end of the game, children can total their purchases and count the amount of money they have left.

○ **Spinners (see page 120):** In addition to using spinners with the game boards, children can create a new game by coloring the spinners as shown. Have groups of two or three play together, each child choosing a color (red, yellow, blue) and guessing how many times the players will spin that color in 10 (or 15, 20, and so on) tries. Children can keep tallies for their colors then make a group graph to show their results.

Compare graphs among groups. Does one color come out a winner each time?

○ **Number Cubes (see page 121):** Help children cut apart and assemble the number cubes, taping tabs together. Keep a basket of cubes handy for a variety of activities, such as:

   ○ Younger students may enjoy tossing cubes 10, 20, or 30 times, and making graphs to record the number that appears on top for each roll. Let children first predict what they think will happen before they begin tossing the cubes.

   ○ More advanced students can toss the cubes, and add, multiply, or subtract the two numbers that appear on top to get an answer closest, for example, to 6.

   ○ Students can toss the number cubes, model the numbers with manipulatives from

Section One, then write addition or subtraction sentences for their models.

○ **Domino Cards (see page 122):** Duplicate three copies of dominoes on heavy paper to make each set. Children can play in pairs or small groups with a domino set. After distributing dominoes among players, children take turns matching the dots as they place the cards in any configuration.

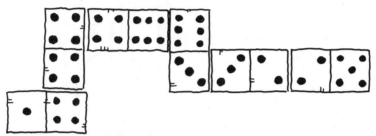

○ **Animal Sets (see pages 123-124):** Children can cut apart and sequence these cards by the numbers they represent. Children will also enjoy using these picture/number cards with Game Board 1 in place of number cubes or spinners.

○ **Finger Puppets (see page 125):** These child-size puppets are favorites for creative play. Children can use them to tell number stories, to act out number rhymes, to explain how they solve problems, to help classmates understand math concepts, and so on. Children may need help in assembling puppets to fit their fingers. Or, let children paste puppets to the tops of sticks to make stick puppets.

○ **Magic Squares (see page 126):** Have children cut apart the numbers at the bottom of the page and manipulate them in the magic squares until each row, column, and diagonal has the same sum. Two solutions are:

4	9	2
3	5	7
8	1	6

16	3	2	13
5	10	11	8
9	6	7	12
4	15	14	1

○ **Teddy Bear Counters (see page 127):** Make a color and counting game by coloring the teddy bears red, yellow, and blue and the spaces on Game Board 1 in corresponding colors. Turn teddy bear counters face down. As children select a counter, they move to the next corresponding color on the game board. Children can also use these as playing pieces for other game or as models for finding solutions to computation problems.

○ **Hooray for You! Award (see page 128):** Children will enjoy receiving this award periodically throughout the year. The award is for math, but a space is available for filling a concept, skill, or understanding (such as fractions, counting from 1 to 10, learning shapes, making patterns, and so on).

Game Board 1

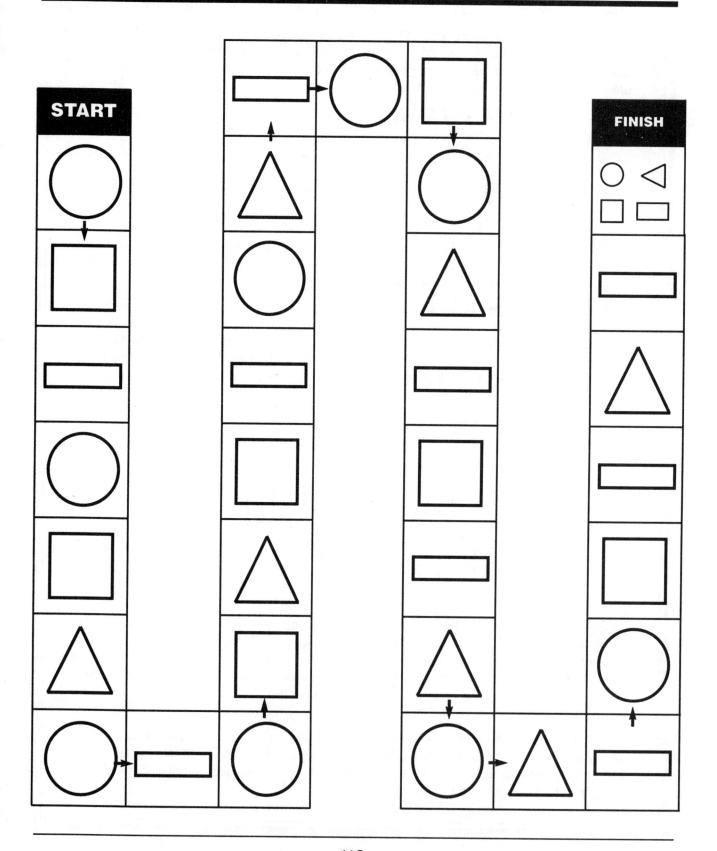

118

Game Board 2

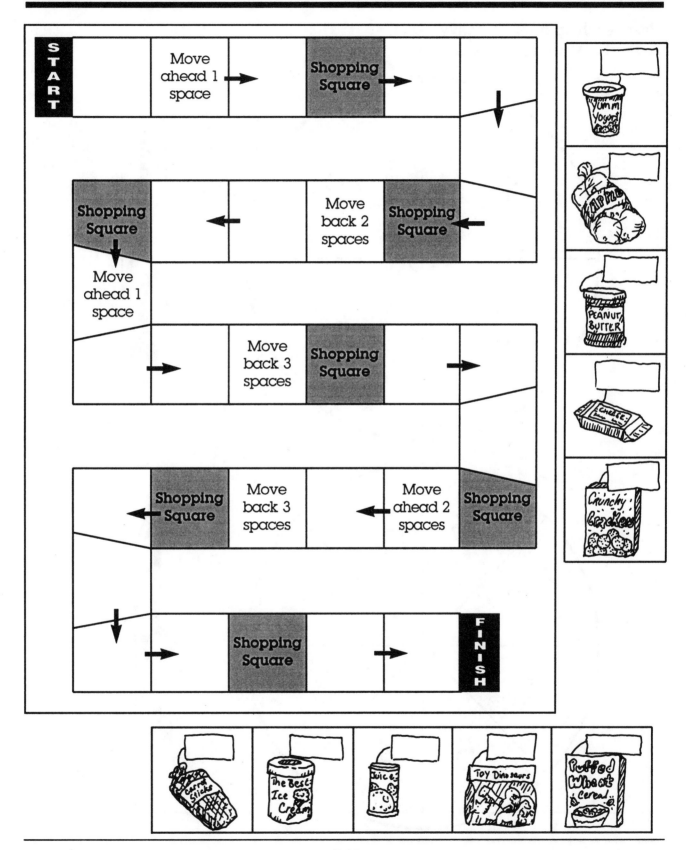

START

Move ahead 1 space

Shopping Square

Shopping Square

Move back 2 spaces

Shopping Square

Move ahead 1 space

Move back 3 spaces

Shopping Square

Shopping Square

Move back 3 spaces

Move ahead 2 spaces

Shopping Square

Shopping Square

FINISH

Spinners

Paste each spinner on heavy paper.
Assemble with a paper fastener.

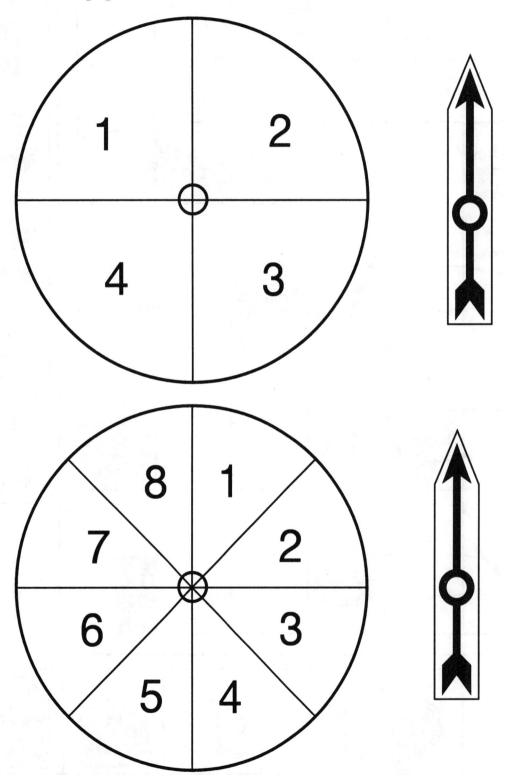

Number Cubes

Cut along solid lines.
Fold along dashed lines.
Tape together to form cubes.

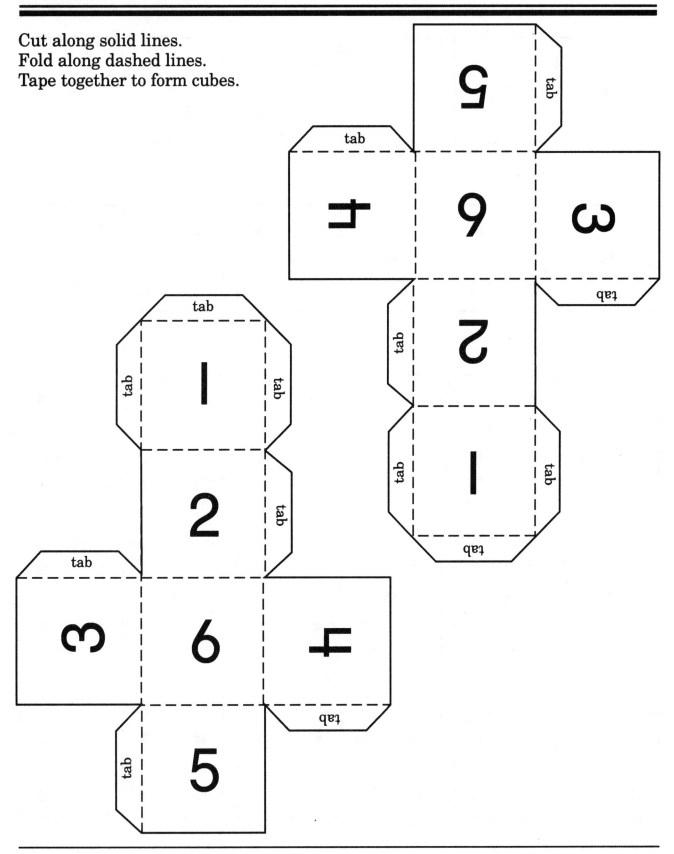

Domino Cards

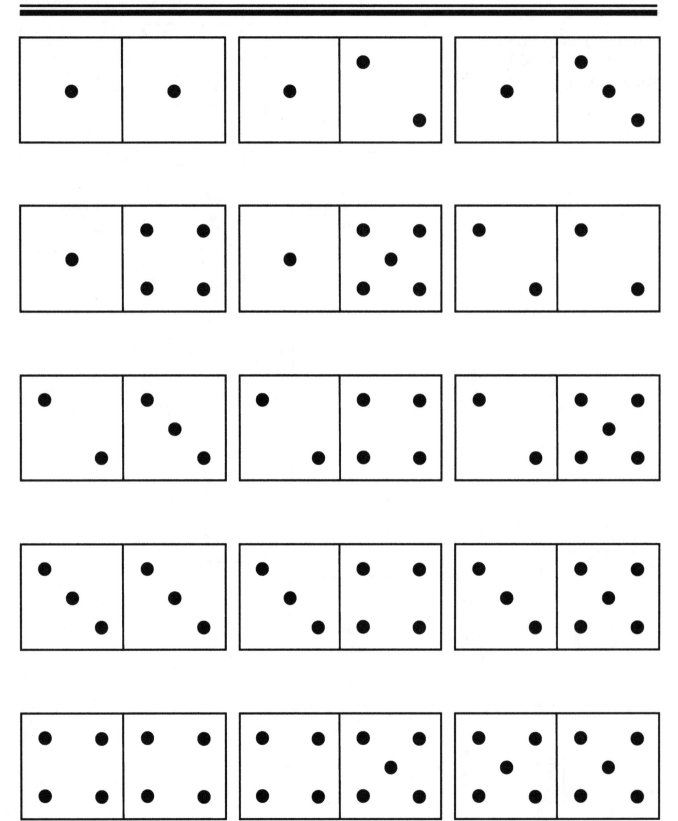

Animal Sets

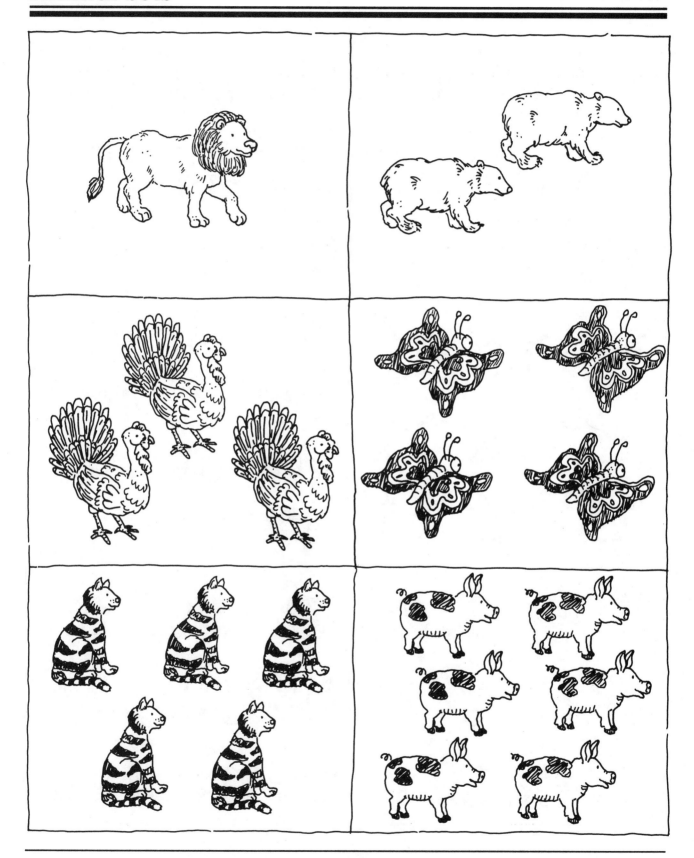

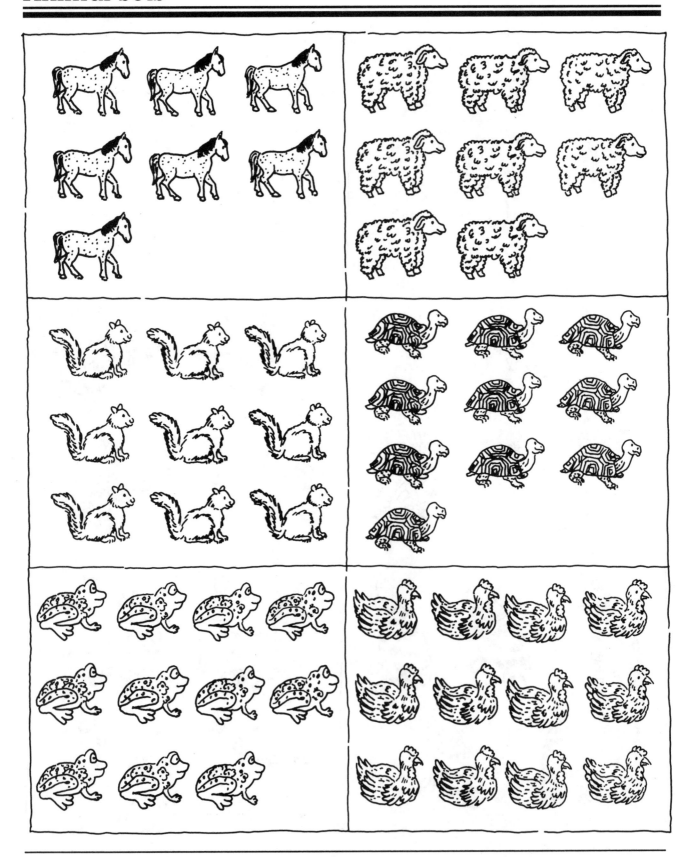

Finger Puppets

Cut apart animal shapes.
Tape side 1 to side 2.
Leave room for your finger.

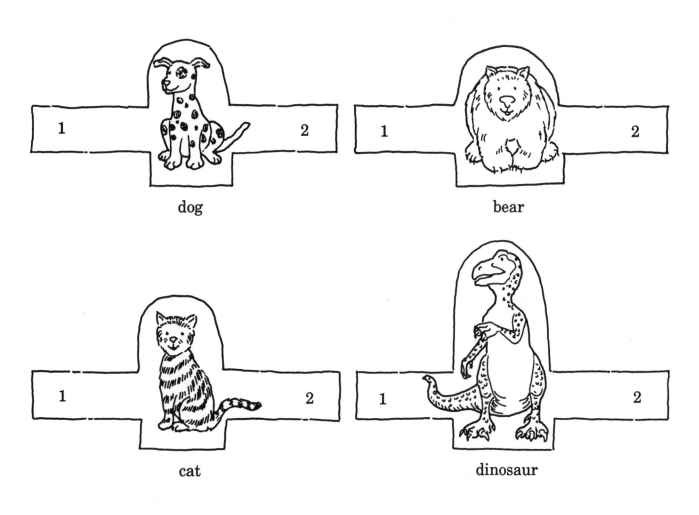

dog

bear

cat

dinosaur

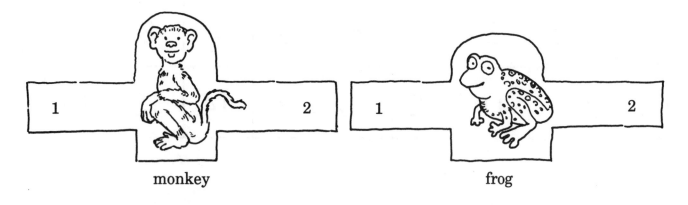

monkey

frog

Magic Squares

Cut out the number pieces.
Arrange the numbers 1 to 9 in Square A.
Arrange the numbers 1 to 16 in Square B.

The numbers in each direction (⟶ , ↓ , and ╱ ╲) must have the same sum.

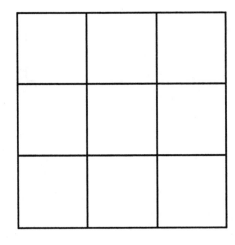

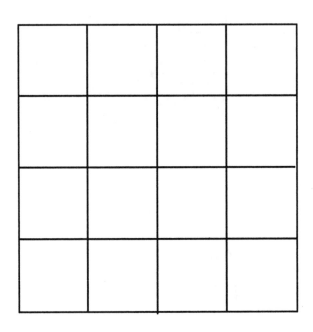

1	2	3	4	5	6	7	8	9
1	2	3	4	5	6	7	8	9
10	11	11	12	13	14	14	15	16

Hooray for You

This award is given to

_____

for marvelous math work in

_____

Date: _____ Signed: _____